ACT AS THOUGH I AM ALREADY, THERE I AM

ACT AS THOUGH I AM ALREADY, THERE I AM

POWER OF THE SPOKEN WORD

Releasing The Grace of God

Julia Byas 3/26/22

JULIA BYAS

XULON PRESS

Xulon Press
2301 Lucien Way #415
Maitland, FL 32751
407.339.4217
www.xulonpress.com

Paperback ISBN-13: 978-1-6628-3633-6
Ebook ISBN-13: 978-1-6628-3634-3

Table of Contents

Apostle Julia Byas,
Senior Pastor, founder

Introducing a trail blazer in her time of ministry, elevating the standard of the holy in the area of presenting the Gospel. She was called into holiness in 1982, alone in her home to be filled with the power of the Holy Ghost. Thereafter, radical changes were displayed in her life. This shocked her dedicated and loving husband Mr. Ben D Byas. He asked her if she was saved and she didn't say a word, knowing that the Holy Spirit instructed her to hold her peace. She changed so much. She was no longer the life of the party and favorite at the clubs, such as Glen Lynn's. God sent His Holy Spirit when she was wearing her red lipstick and red nail polish, tight jeans and mink coat -- dressed to impress, sitting on a bar stool where she was friends to many. God chose Julia to be a pioneer and innovator to raise the standards of holiness, a widow in a man's world. She is now walking into 73 years young on a fast track, empowered to write about her new life style, being in God and holding on until Jesus comes. In her new book, she is walking from the beginning of the prophetic words spoken and erasing all the negative words spoken over her life. No man can take credit, but so many have spoken into her life before and after the death of her precious son Apostle Maurice Olden Lewis, son of Mr. Martin Olden Lewis, her childhood husband at 17 years old. Truly, Julia was called from darkness to His marvelous light and was clothed with righteousness to blaze a trail of holiness. Welcome to her journey and recognize the Power of Our Spoken Words. Holding On is her heart's desire...

Introduction

Stand Still and See

"Ye shall not need to fight in this battle: set yourselves,
stand ye still, and see the salvation of the Lord with you"
(2Chronicles 20:17).

This is a story about Apostle Julia Byas, founder of Immanuel Temple-God with us/ Women of Power Ministry/Servants Working in Unity/Talking With Power.

Julia was born March 11, 1948. She grew up in a lower middle-class home. She paid her way through Saint Henry Catholic School on California Street in South St. Louis Missouri. This was after her mother was no longer able to pay for her education. Her parish priest, Father Kemp, assisted her in finding a job at the church cleaning the benches and was her support from 5th until 8th grade. Julia learned to take care of business at an early age. This was her foundation. Julia graduated with honors from nursing RN/ASD/CCRN/CIVT in December of 1977 with her precious husband Ben D Byas at her side, cheering her every step of her journey. She worked as a nurse for more than 49.5 years and retired from nursing at age sixty. She was awarded Outstanding International Nursing 2009, Woman of the Year 2009, and received many accolades for her success in nursing including Outstanding from VAMC for performance.

Julia married Ben Byas, her true inspiration in this journey called life. Julia's first husband, Martin, was her heartbeat, widowed at 21 years of age. She gave birth to two lovely children. Mr. Martin Olden Lewis was her first love.

Julia remained a Catholic for 33+ years until in 1982 when she encountered the power of the Holy Spirit in her home. This was evidenced by speaking in tongues and the rest is history. She walked with her Lord and journeyed with God who compelled her to write. You will hear more as you thumb through the pages of her life. There is Power in The Spoken Word/Talking With Power.

Chapter One

Your Thoughts Become Things

W e cannot always control our thoughts; however, we can control our words. Eventually, words impress upon the subconscious and impact our future. That is why mastering our thoughts is so important. I hope my writing will help us to understand the nature or meaning of what we say. We must understand how our speech impacts what we receive. Each of us must take total responsibility for what we experience in our lives. We are responsible for every choice that we make and what we allow to occur in our own lives. If we do not like what we see, the choice is there to make a change. We can decide to change direction by the words we speak. We can change the outcome of our future. I hope my journey can shine a light on how I awoke with confidence in the Word of God that brought me to a place of total dependence on Elohim. We must come to the understanding the we, personally, are responsible to make changes in our lives. If we want to see victory, real talk comes from our relationship with God. In this process, we are aligning our thoughts the Word of God. "I will put my instructions deep within them, and I will write them on their hearts." (Jer. 31:33 NLT). Our power source is the Word of God. We can obtain this understanding by studying and yielding to the Word. The spiritually awakened person is not too good to be true. The absolute truth is in God we trust. "My thoughts are not your thoughts, neither are your ways my ways, saith the Lord" (Isa. 55:8). We must thirst for the water of the spirit that can quench the inner thirst for righteousness. "The thirst not of wine and milk. Say there is anyone thirsty? Come and drink even if you have no money, come, take your choice of wine and milk it's all free. Why spend money on food that doesn't give you strength? Why pay for groceries that do you no good? Listen and I'll tell you where to get food that will fatten your soul. But hearken diligently unto the Lord, eat ye that which is good and let your soul be fatten". (Isa. 55:1-2). Here, the author explains that the word of God nourishes us and keeps us strong. We should continue to say what God says in order to change our thoughts to His thoughts and complete this chosen journey. (v5) Come to the Lord willing to hear and yielded, listen for good counsel in the word of God. Your soul is at stake your mind your will and emotions) God is ready to make an everlasting covenant with us, said the Lord in (v3) To give you my mercies that He had given King David. (v5) You will also command nations, they will come running to obey not because of your own power or virtue, but because I the Lord your God have glorified you (v6) Seeking the Lord while you can find him ,call upon him now, when he allow you to hear.(v7) Cast off the thoughts of doing wrong. Then turn to the Lord and receive His mercy. He will abundantly pardon. The plan of God is not for us to exercise our willful nature. "For just as the heavens are higher than the earth so are my ways higher than yours said the Lord" (Isa 55:9). We must thirst for the food of the Spirit that can quench that inner thirst for righteousness. I had one of my young mentee's tell me he always believed that God was present in his life, regardless of his location. He trusted the Word as he learned in his youth that God was real. When he stepped back into the kingdom, he was able to take giant steps into his deliverance. He walked straight into his destiny, set by his Savior, the Almighty God. He was able to trust God as he proceeded into the wonderful experience of divine deliverance. We can start strong; but really the key is to stay delivered, holding fast to whom we belong and not to ourselves. Before we, as yielded vessels of God can be used as a mouthpiece, we must allow our hearts to be changed. In mid-June of 1982, I confessed with my mouth and believed in my heart Jesus was my Lord and Savior asking my Adoni to change my life. Immediately there was a total change in the woman who had her own plans. My immediate family was my total focus prior to my conversion with my Adoni. The words I spoke that night while awakening from sleep created a desire to change my life. I heard a strong tongue coming out of my mouth, filling me with a new awareness of who I was. The day before I had asked God to take the taste of sin from my life while in the car with my husband. I remember that day clearly, we headed north on Page Avenue passing a church called Westside. Later in my ministry, I had the pleasure to work with the pastor of that church to conduct weeks of revival. God is miraculous! Many were saved and we saw miracles of healing with the Apostle from Road Island who led the meetings. Powerful words of deliverance were spoken in my life and others. Before this time, I was sick with high blood pressure and back pain. God healed me, and I am now walking in my deliverance. At those meetings, I was in charge every Thursday night and I received much encouragement which strengthened me in my ministry and as a leader in the community. I made many connections which helped my future in our community. The Lord said I will put my law in their inward parts and write it in their hearts, and I will be their God and they shall be my people(.Jeremiah 31:33) I have received many impartations since that wonderful day of conversation with my Lord in prayer. And they shall teach no more every man his neighbor, every man his brother saying, know the Lord; for they shall all know me.(v.33:34) We all can have the blessing of knowing God through yielding to the Holy Spirit, the person. By His spirit, the Voice of God came to empower us as believers to know and recognize the voice of God. This process is available for all who believe and trust in the work of the cross. Let's take this moment to rededicate our hearts to Adoni and accept a deeper revelation of His power. **THOUGHTS BECOME THINGS. IF YOU RECEIVE IT IN YOUR MIND YOU WILL HOLD YOUR DELIVERANCE IN YOU HEART AND RETURN IT BACK TO THE LORD IN PRAISE AND THANKSGIVING. RECEIVE TODAY IN THE MIGHTY NAME OF JESUS.**

Only our doubts, fears and resentments keep positive things or good times from us. In my walk with the Lord, I have had many negative events. During my journey at the first church after leaving my roots as a catholic, I was told continuously across the pulpit that women could not be called to preach the gospel; but there was a pulling in my heart that I could not shake. I went to my pastor and he gave me an assignment to do the prayer line that was attached to my home line. My whole family was involved with this assignment and we were stuck there for years. My personal call almost died. Our Lord is direct when He calls us. He will send words of encouragement from many to move us in the right direc-tion -- to our destiny. I was under a controlling ministry when the Lord got my attention. The more I studied and learned who He was, the more the soft still voice of calling began to manifest the Chosen One within me. One day in prayer, I was asked from my innermost being "were women able to preach"? A knowing was in my heart. I began my own research and the rest is history. I was on a journey of truth that spoke many changes in my life and I evolved into a totally yielded holy vessel of light to draw others, one person at time, to Adoni. I yielded to receive the total package set before us in God. I was called in 1992; but did not accept my full calling as a pastor until 2001. I did not look back and meditated over hard times. We should hold on as we are drawn into the presence that allows us to focus on our destiny. I trusted God who had taken total control and opened my understanding. When we allow Him to be Lord over our lives, the spoken word has power for Godly and ungodly purposes. The whole universe came forward through words. God spoke the world into existence in Genesis 1. Death and life are in the power of the tongue (Prov. 18:21). Right words are weighty, intense, impressive, powerful, valid and energetic. At the right time they carry tremendous power and force to the hearer. Give thanks for a new day. Become immune to all discouragement and adverse appearance of defeat. Psalm 27 awakens us as we read and receive His word. "The Lord is our light and our salvation, whom shall we fear? The Lord is strength of our life of whom shall we be afraid. He has already covered the wickedness of our mind to line up our thoughts to Him with. When the wicked, even mine enemies and foes, come upon me up my flesh they slumber and fell. Yes, though a mighty army marches against me, my heart shall know no fear! I am confident that God will save me. We declare victory in every area of our life now in the mighty name of Jesus Christ the son of the living God. I shall not fear, in His will we be confident. One thing we desire of the Lord, that will we seek after, that we may dwell in the house of the Lord all the days of our life, to behold the beauty of the Lord, and enquire in His temple" (Psalm 27 1-14).

All that we desire or require is already on our path, but we must be wide awake to our good life in God. In order to bring an event, action, or object into full manifestation, we speak life, then we will realize or even feel ourself in a new environment. "Waiting on the Lord we shall be of good courage, and He shall strengthen thine heart wait I say on the Lord". (Psalm 27:14). As the old negative condition falls away, we will continue to speak, then we will receive abundant life in Jesus Name we declare now.

The thief cometh not, but for to steal, and to kill, and to destroy I am come that they might have life, and that they might have it more abundantly. (John 10:10) I started my church as pastor in 2001. I would not have believed that I would lose my immediate family over this. Remember, my immediate family was my focus at salvation. I started with my heart directed toward obedience to the call. I understand the enemy is working his plan; but I firmly believe that my Lord is in total control of my destiny. I am a family person; so therefore, I am family centered. As my congregation continued to grow in front of my eyes, I expected the call to change my life. I am still family focused, finding myself today doing the same thing with my church *family*. My immediate family had decided to disconnect from the church family, some having house church with no leader and some no church, speaking against my commitment to God. They verbalized openly that I was putting the church before them. I am growing in my relationship with my Adoni daily. My church family is still receiving the benefits from my walk. My immediate family are still making decisions not to follow Christ, which has caused a break in our fellowship as a strong family unit. The church family is growing and receiving all the miracles of our commitment. As a church family, we see miracles, signs and wonders daily (to God be all the Glory). When I first received the call and was chosen, I was totally changed and focused on building my relationship with Him. I kept my immediate family in the center and most events were centered around them. We still invite them, but they don't show. They continue to say that I am putting the church first. I am hopeful they will read my book. My granddaughter, Faith, told me "granny tell your story". With the Lord's help, I am telling my story. I am putting God first so that all will received His blessing. We are changing lives -- one life at a time. We are keeping our congregation holy family centered and it is working. We welcome new members into the holy family. We, as a family, help drug addicts, alcoholics, gender confusion, marriages, homelessness, etc. -- all sins are addressed. God has shown us how to help the helpless and our family is growing in victory through Him. Trust the words that He is speaking into your life. Study the word of God and totally depend on what He is saying to you by revelation, the revealed word of God. See John 10:10. God has given revelation to our pulpit and brought much deliverance to the hurting in the church. Jesus promised the abundant life in the above scripture. We ask ourselves, how can we experience lasting joy, peace and purpose in a world often covered and controlled by discouragement and fear? Having abundant life means to have a supernatural life; a superabundance of a thing; a life with fullness of joy; and strength for your spirit soul and body. It is an inspiration from God the father, through the door of Jesus Christ our savior. God brings abundant blessings for the yielded to dwell in abundance; it means we have everything we need in life -- more than enough. To be blessed abundantly in this life means we are full on every side to the glory of our Lord. We receive as we obey the word of His commandments -- by grace we are saved. We continue to see the Lord give homes to the homeless, jobs to the jobless, etc. He helps our people persevere and deals with the whole man which is a blessing. Jesus is so unlike the thief who comes to steal, kill and destroy. Jesus comes with abundant life. The Greek word for abundant can also mean excess, more than, or superfluous. A sinful nature means flesh, many times used to describe the human body. Your sinful nature has been forgiven and that means you have become a slave to righteousness. For the Law of the Spirit of life has set you free in Christ from the law of sin and death. Salvation is the center of our ministry and we are seeing many change their lives. We are called in the Lord as slave is to a freedman of the Lord. We are called out of darkness into His marvelous light. Sin mean wicked, such as to make one feel guilty -- a sinful act. Apostle Paul declared: It is for freedom that

Christ has set us free (Gal.5:1) That freedom for me is obedience to the call on my life.

"Study to shew thyself approved unto God a workman that needeth not be ashamed, rightly dividing the word of truth." (2 Timothy 2:15 KJV). The bible teaches that God is sovereign and that is the essential aspect of who He is. He has supreme authority in all things and yes, He is very much active, despite our inability to understand. As Paul wrote, "God works all things according to the counsel of his will" (Eph.1:11).

The Importance of truth. Truth matters, to us as individuals and to our society as whole. Truth is wisdom and walking in wisdom is truth manifested. As individuals this means that we can grow and mature, learning from our mistakes. For society, truthfulness creates social bonds; whereas being a liar and being a hypocrite breaks them. Truth is when you totally yield to the call. Being chosen, you will be accused wrongly and unjustly, because some will not understand your commitment to the call. Not your will but His will for your life. Have your assurance heavenly focused. Society places a high value on truth, it is the foundation for a fair and just society. In court rooms, we are required to swear to tell the truth as a witness on the stand. Most religions place a higher value on truth or the principles of truthfulness. I am hoping that this statement stands true in our society today. In the last four years, we have seen truth twisted in our nation's high places of power. We declare in the name of Jesus that truth will rise and stand tall in our churches and in our society -- in the mighty name we declare in Jesus now. We in the kingdom of God must display stability to make quality decisions. To change how we speak, we must consider our honesty and evaluate our attributes such as integrity, truthfulness, and straightforwardness (including our conduct, absence of lying, cheating and stealing). Honesty also involves being trustworthy, loyal, fair and sincere. These attributes must be cultivated in our walk with our Creator and maintained in our high standards of holiness. There is a difference between truth and honesty. Being honest means not telling lies; whereas being truthful means actively making known all truth of the matter. But, if they unknowingly say something that isn't true, they are still being honest. This suggests you can be honest without telling the truth. With this statement revealed, we must study the Word with diligence to seek the truth so that we would at all cost speak the truth. Having knowledge of truth is important in our journey to build God's kingdom on the earth. "And ye shall know the truth, and the truth shall make you free." (John 8:32). Working as leader and a woman of God, I was accused of giving all my money to the congregation and not unto God – that is their truth. When we are called, it is a call unto our Savior, then He does the rest. Lies will be spoken, but we as a family in the kingdom hold our truth in Him and allow Him to fight our battles. Everything that we give to God is directed back to His people and we are blessed as we continue to give Him our life. To all Glory unto our God.

WARFARE, PRAYER IS OUR WEAPON
The power of the spirit is mighty even unto the pulling down strongholds.

For the weapons of our warfare are not carnal; but mighty through God to pull down a strong hold. The victory is won by God within the subconscious of a renewed mind. "Let this mind be in you which is also in Christ Jesus" (Phil.2:5). Let everyone see that you are unselfish and considerate in all you do. Don't worry about anything; instead, pray about everything. Tell God your needs, and don't forget to thank Him for His answers. We find ourselves asking Him why we must experience so much pain in this walk from the ones closest to us. Always provide a comforting response quickly about your Savior. If you do this, you will experience God's peace, which is far more wonderful than the human mind can understand.

His peace will keep your thoughts and your hearts quiet and provide rest as you trust in Christ Jesus. "Whatever things are true, whatever things are honest, whatever things are just, whatever things are pure whatever are lovely, whatever things are of a good report, if there be any virtue, high moral standards, and there be any praise, think on these things" (Phil 4:8). Obey and speak the Word of God. Obedience starts with my made-up mind. "We all have free will unto our Lord. Always be full of joy in the Lord, I say it again rejoice" (Phil 4:4). When we are fighting for what we believe, we must continue to give Him thanks and praise. Hold on to your testimonies. We are overcomers! "And they overcame him by the blood of the lamb, and by the word of their testimony: and they loved not their lives unto the death" (Rev.12:11). The testimony is revelation of God. It represents God's heart desire which is also God's requirement, or we may say, God's standard. His standard reveals Himself, showing us what a great God He is. When this testimony comes to man, it becomes law. Personal testimony is simply the Good news presented in terms of your own experience. It is sharing where your life and God's action have intersected. "Blessed are the undefiled in the way, who walk in the law of Lord. Blessed are they that keep his testimonies, and that seek him with the whole heart"(Ps.119:1-2). They also do no iniquity as they walk in his ways. This is a testimony of Jesus in your life. "I will speak of thy testimonies also before kings, and will not be ashamed" (Ps.119:46).

"And if it seem evil unto to serve the Lord, choose you this day whom ye will serve; whether the gods which your father severed that were on the other side of the flood, or whose land ye dwell: but as for me and my house, we will serve the Lord." (Joshua 24:15). We must choose to serve the Lord by faith. We hold onto that choice when the enemy comes to test our faith with doubt and trials. Hold on to the word that has been imparted in your heart by the Word of God. Trust God and His word by faith and meditate on His word. Declare the blood of Jesus covers. That is warfare, prayer is warfare, and the word and praise is warfare against the enemy. Picture your-self in victory and see yourself finished. Denounce injustice con-cerning things in your life. **"Rejoice in the Lord always; and again I say rejoice"** (Phil. 4:4).

DESTROYING THE IMAGE OF POVERTY IN YOUR LIFE

"And He called the multitude and said unto them, Hear, and understand. Not that which goeth into the mouth defileth a man; but that which cometh out of the mouth, this defileth a man. Then came his disciples, and said unto him. Knowest thou that the Pharisees were offended, after they heard this saying? But He answered and said, every plant, which my heavenly Father hath not planted, shall be rooted up. Let them alone; they be blind leaders of blind. And if the blind lead the blind both shall fall into the ditch" (Matthew 15: 10-14).

Jesus promised us that the Father will remove the things in our mind that did not come from Him. Defeat, poverty, lack, sorrow, pain, sin, destruction, deceptions, lies and confusion. When we read, "For out of the heart proceed evil thoughts, murders, adul-teries, fornications, thieves, false witness, blasphemies. These are the things which defile a man; but to eat with unwashed hands defileth not a man." (Matthew 15:19-20). To be able to see yourself successful you must have your mind, heart and your subconscious renewed. It has to change by faith. What you are accustomed to must be rooted in the word of God. We already have the promises of our savior Jesus Christ. Now we need a new mind of faith that believes in the miracles of God. Every time we attempt to climb out, the enemy of our mind pulls us back. We must refuse to continue to walk in this flow of poverty. The book of Jeremiah 1:9 says, "The Lord has said that Behold I have put my words in thy mouth." We must always say the words of the Lord. "I have this day set thee over the nations and over the Kingdoms to root out and put; down, and to destroy, and throw down, to build and to plant." (Jeremiah 1:10). Our subconscious is designed to keep us in a comfort zone; but we must allow the word of God to come into our heart and destroy the image of poverty that has been built into our mind and the mind of the church. Let's be healed in the mighty name of Jesus.

WISDOM AND UNDERSTANDING

The beginning of wisdom is the fear of the Lord. Wisdom is the ability to think and act using knowledge, experience, understanding, common sense and insight. Wisdom defines knowledge and capacity to make use of it. I was told all my life that I was a person of wisdom. Growing closer to God, I see myself understanding what wisdom is. During counseling, my mentees receive revelation about their problems, then we see the miracles of His mighty hand at work. We have experienced great accomplishments from one-on-one sessions at our church, and feel this is the direction the Lord is leading us as a ministry. Wisdom is supreme; therefore get wisdom though it at all cost -- let's get understanding. Through understanding and truth we are able to use common sense with the knowledge that God has manifested deliverance to His people. I followed my new heart and believed in the destiny of our ministry persevering -- the vision God gave me in 1982. When my husband was addicted, my life was in a spiral of defeat. I had to totally depend on the wisdom of God to help with his addiction cycle. I joined a class and sat in proxy for him. Later, I became a teacher and led the class. I was then promoted to Pastor for seven years, and he became my student. We thank our Lord Jesus for saving him. Recognizing that there was a problem began my wise journey. I acknowledged and accepted that I could not control the problem; but rather, let request be made known unto God. "Be careful for nothing; but in everything by prayer and supplication with thanksgiving let your requests be made known to God." (Phil.

4:6). I prayed every morning after working the night shift as an RN in 2000. I found the peace of God in His presence. He was my sustainer. I rejoiced praying to God.

Paul the Apostle stated, "And the peace of God, which passeth all understanding, shall keep your hearts and minds through Christ Jesus." (Phil 4:7). Paul continued, "...those things, which ye have both learned, and received, and heard, and seen in me, do and the God of peace shall be with you." (Phil 4:9). "I can do all things through Christ which strengthen me." (Phil 4:13). As Paul was on his journey, he reflected that we must trust God, as he was not anxious for anything, we should also trust God. He said in Philippians 4:19-20 "But my God shall supply all your needs according to His riches in glory by Christ Jesus. Giving God praise on his journey. Now unto God and our Father be glory forever and ever." We who are saints should avoid being anxious and trust the divine plan of God through His word. During this time in my life, I received so many spoken words that I was able to stay connected and walk closely with my Savior as a witness that He is a God of peace.

Without vision, my people would perish in lack and limitation. As a congregation we are not experiencing lack and we give God praise. We see the glory of God manifested in our church every time we enter. Without vision, we may work hard and accomplish nothing and question where we are headed. We need a road map, a vision, to clearly know where we are going. We need to keep our eyes focused on the goal to finish the race. Who believes in you? Find them then agree together. If you believe in yourself, others will also believe in you. In Matt. 18:19-20 it is written, "Again I say unto you, that if two of you shall agree on earth as touching anything that they shall ask, it shall be done for them of my Father which is in heaven. For where two or three are gathered together in my name, there am I in the midst of them."

I was always told unity is power -- thank you Lord for the power of unity expressed. My testimony is God has blessed me with a wonderful loving congregation that has been in agreement with me for over twenty years. We have survived the hardship of this pandemic declared on March 12,2020. We continued to worship and grow mighty in His presence. I have been inspired to write and start new ministries. During the pandemic, we have helped four young people go to college. Our financial portfolio stabilized. We were instructed in prayer by the guidance of the Holy Spirit to take communion weekly. It has been a wonderful experience obeying God in a crisis. Amos asked, "Can two walked together, except they be agreed?" (Amos 3:3). Marriage is the most powerful unity that needs agreement to last with full success. The marriage unit must be in total agreement to walk in Godly wisdom and understand the Word of God for great accomplishment. Christ is married to the church we are His bride. And "as the bridegroom rejoiceth over the bride, so shall thy God rejoice over thee." (Isa. 62:5).

As you continue to trust and believe in yourself and the Holy Spirit within you, anxiousness and fear will leave your heart and mind. With the divine guidance of the Holy Spirit, the wind will shift you into purpose. Our Lord within protects, guides and provides when we fully trust. Make a quality decision to allow God complete control over your life through the dictates of His Word. Most people lose because they fear loss. They take unnecessary precautions, not trusting the Protector, the Eye who watches over Israel. Put whatever you love under the law of divine protection, then rest. Jesus said, "come to me, all of you who are weary and carry heavy burdens, and I will give you rest. Take my yoke upon you. Let me teach you, because I am humble and gentle at heart, and you will give rest for your souls. For my yoke is easy to bear, and the burden I give you is light." (Matthew 11:28-30).

Chapter Two

Our Walk With Jehoshaphat

My focus was torn between two families. As a leader called to a people, I kept prayer at the root to hold us together. I have studied Jehoshaphat, who was a divided king, constantly balancing his leadership role with pressures of outside influence. I was constantly wrongly accused of putting my congregation first. They did not understand that my commitment was not to a people; but rather, with my Lord and Savior. In my study, I am encouraged to be courageous in the Lord. I am not afraid or discouraged. I must depend on the strength of the Holy Spirit. For the battle belongs to God and I continue to rely on the spirit of God which allows me to handle the outside trauma in this season of victory. The attacks are real from the spoken word to actions. Having faith and listening to the voice of God has strengthened me in this holy walk with my Creator. I use the Word for building an army and forts to hold up the ministry that has been handed to me by my Lord as I lead with excellence. I Campaign against idolatry and for the continuous worship of the only true God. I speak life to establish leaders in the prophetic school in process since 2015 (and as we continue our deliverances started in 1997). I also conduct drug rehab classes. These are the roots of my ministry -- to educate the people about God's laws with the ability to travel outside of Immanuel Temple God worship center and survive. As a survivor in leadership, I am trusting Him to bring me to His expected end. In 2 Chronicles 20:12, Jehoshaphat addresses God. He Recognizes there is a problem and he is coming to his God for the answer; but first he must recognize that his God is a powerful judge. Knowing our Lord is a requirement to approach Him. Jehoshaphat prayed and called his people together. He asked God for the answers to win the battle that was approaching. He asked: "Our God, will thou not judge them? For we have no might against this great company that cometh against us, neither know we what to do, but eyes are upon thee." (2 Chronicles 20:12). At this point, all power comes from our Lord. We must recognize and acknowledge our weakness in the presence of our God, open the door of our faith and totally depend on His words. In 2 Chronicles 13:14, "All Judah stood before the Lord with little ones, their wives, and their children. Upon the son, a Levite of sons of Asaph came the Spirit of the Lord in the midst of the congregation."

In the above passage, **the Lord is speaking** in the midst of his people. This is prophetic to me in the midst of us seeking Him. He speaks and give us direction on how to defeat our enemy. As a group of people coming together every prayer time, we have experienced the glory of God in our church. Surely unity is power. Thus said the Lord unto you, "be not afraid nor dismayed by reason of this great multitude, for the battle is not yours, but God's this is a command from the Lord." (2 Chronicles 20:15). When we, as His chosen get His attention, promises of God are ye and Amen. When we moved in our new building 2017 we experienced a lot of gun shots outside our parking lot. We had to hire security to watch the cars. There were a lot of homeless who would walk in; but through prayer, the Mayor reported that crime to our county. Instruction: "tomorrow go ye down against them, and ye shall find them at the end of the brook before the wilderness of Jeruel. Ye shall not need to fight in this battle set yourselves, stand ye still, and see the salvation of the Lord with you. Juda band Jerusalem fear not, not be dismayed, tomorrow go out against them for the Lord will be with you" (2Chronicles 20:16-17). Waiting on God to move takes faith and time in our process of getting to that place of totally yielding to His manifested presence in our lives. Hold on to the process of prayer in victory. "And Jehoshaphat bowed his head with his face to the ground and all Judah and the inhabitants of and fell before the Lord, worshiping the Lord" (2 Chronicles 20:18). "They rose early in the morning and forth into the wilderness of Tekoa. Jehoshaphat stood and said, hear me o Judah and ye inhabitants of Jerusalem. Believe in the Lord, and that should praise the beauty of holiness, as they went out before the army and say 'praise the Lord for His mercy endureth forever'. And when they begin to sing and to praise the Lord set an ambush against the children the enemy and they were smitten."

(2 Chronicles 20:20-22). They destroyed each other. Praise is an expression of warm approval or admiration of someone or something. In the bible, the definition of praise is the act of expressing approval or admiration, commendation and laudation. It is the offering of grateful homage in words or song, as an act of worship: a hymn of praise to God. The true meaning in dictionary, praise is defined as an expression of one's gratitude and respect towards a deity, especially in song. So, Christian praise can be defined as the expression of reverence toward God, especially in a song. The purpose of praise, admiration or approval is when you're on the receiving end of it you feel great. Whether it is used as a verb or a noun, praise means approval. An example of praise is giving God all the praise in words and song. When we

praise the Lord, we are magnifying Him and putting every other thing below Him. When we praise, we shift our attention from ourselves, other people, and all that is happening around us, to God. We, as believers, experience the presence of God which may result in limitless favor (encouragement, healing, deliverance, joy, peace and provision). Again, the most important reason to praise God includes the fact that He is worthy and that God takes pleasure in our praise. We say to our God in praise that we honor Him for His goodness and power. In our prayer, we say: Lord it is so amazing that you are so powerful that you my Lord created the heavens and the earth; yet you still care about someone as small as me; Lord I give you all the praise for my new life in You; In God I move and have my being, without you Lord I am nothing, thank you, Lord; we, praise and worship You in prayer that we may communicate with You Lord. This is a time to approach God, not because we have another set of needs; but just because we want to praise Him for His works or adore Him for His attributes. Praise is also warfare. Your praise will confuse the enemy when you are in trouble as you begin to give God praise. Praise and worship breaks yokes and brings deliverance. The enemy loves when we focus on our problems (what someone said or did to us) and not upon God, as that is when the enemy can infiltrate our minds and put thoughts in it that will hold us captive. Know that God is literally present, bow down low before Him in your soul, mind, spirit and body when you can. We are the temple of God according to Christ Jesus. Sing worship songs or hymns for the Lord. Pray to the Lord, thanking Him for His many good blessings. It brings us joy and draws us closer to our God. Some people value specific timely praise. What did He do? When did it happen? For grace we give God praise. Take time to listen. Spring into action and just give Him thanks. Give to God His gift of praise, then continue to stay in a place of adoration. It completes us in Him. God's love for us brings good. Praise confuses the enemy. For this reason, it is an effective weapon. We can fight the enemy and even our own negative feelings with praise. Praise creates an atmosphere for the Holy Spirit to work and move and for God to answer prayers. The Lord says: Do not be afraid! Do not be discouraged by this mighty army, for the battle is not yours, but God's. See 2 Chronicles 15. Praise your way to victory. It confuses the enemy and it allows God to demonstrate His mighty power on our behalf. So powerful is the praise of our Lord's chosen people so let us continue to give Him praise. "And when Judah came toward the watch tower in the wilderness, they looked unto the multitude and behold ,they were dead bodies fallen to earth and none escaped" (2 Chronicles 20:24). "And when Jehoshaphat and his people came to take away the spoil of them, they found among them in abundance both riches with dead bodies and precious jewels, which they stripped off from themselves, more than they could carry away" (2 Chronicles 20:25). Abundance of blessings are manifested when we follow the Lord's direction. Catch this statement right here! "And they were three days in gathering of the spoil it was so much. For the Lord had made them to rejoice over their enemies" (2 Chronicles 20:27). In Exodus, the scripture states, "The Lord is my strength and my song; He has given me victory. This is my God, and I will praise Him my Father's God, and I will exalt Him!" (Exodus 15:2). In Psalms it states, "The Lord is a refuge for the oppressed a stronghold in times of trouble" (Ps.9:9-10); and "Those who seek the Lord lack no good thing" (Ps.34:10). Consequently, the realm of Jehoshaphat was quiet for his God gave him rest. Giving God no thanks, we become ungrateful, or we give thanks to others for our blessings, or we take credit for things ourselves. When we lose our focus on God and thanking God, it distorts us spiritually in our minds and hearts. That's why we need to give thanks- it is for our own well-being. **In praise the people helped and were** able to assist the king in completing his duties as a king in peace. He reigned 25 years in Jerusalem. Jehoshaphat acted as a righteous King at 35 years of age and a man of prayer and obedience, in the midst of fear he received VICTORY.

Chapter Three

Seek Ye First

"But seek ye first the kingdom of God, and his righteousness; and all these things shall be added unto you" **(Matthew 6:33).**

Our job as leaders in the kingdom is to make sure that we stay connected to our Creator by seeking the presence of God in much prayer and supplication unto Him. We must maintain an environment that is conducive for His PRESENCE.

PEACE AND PROSPERITY

Jesus said, "come to me all ye that are weary and heavy laden and I will give you rest." (Matthew 11:28). Let us REST in the Word of God. He was speaking of the Christ within, your super-conscious mind, (the renewal of the mind) where there are no burdens and no worries. Doubts, fears and negativity are in the subconscious. Only our emotions keep us from reaping our harvest of success -- happiness and abundance. In 1982, I received the call of the Holy Spirit at my home. I had been in the Catholic church all my life and this was my first encounter in the realm of the Spirit. I learned the voice of God as a child. I was a loner and frequently experienced divine revelation. I was not aware of what God was doing. I always gave account that my angels were with me at all times. I was not knowledgeable of the Holy Spirit as the third divine person of holy trinity. "I will restore to you the years the locusts have eaten, the caterpillar and the palmerworm, my great army which I sent among you" (Joel 2:25). What a powerful statement. I thank God for restoration in my journey. I lost so many family and friends when I accepted my call as pastor. In a male dominated world, I had no bible to understand their actions. Thank God that I had a personal encounter and had a relationship with my Lord so I was sensitive to His voice. I depended totally on His word; and with time in God's presence, I grew closer in my walk. Now is my season to receive from all the pain and for my suffering. It cannot be compared to the Glory that is being revealed in my life now. I am so impressed with my Lord. He is making me cry and laugh at the same time. I give Glory to His wonderful Name -- Jesus is my Lord and Savior.

The promise of God is His word. When we receive the Holy Spirit, there is a feeling of wellness. Some examples are: social; responsibility; optimism; contributing to optimism; connectedness with others; feelings of belonging, and being in love with self. These qualities will allow you to be used in the Kingdom of God. Restoration is truly a part of God's Kingdom. Our responsibility is to develop our spiritual life after being filled at salvation. Explore your spiritual core. Look deep and search the Word for answers to obtain a deeper meaning. Think positive, we know from the Word that what a man thinks so is he. Speak positive, remember words have power. Take time to meditate on the Word of God. Read and study so that you will divide the Word properly and apply it to your daily walk with your Creator. Think on these things as true, honest, just, pure, lovely and His good report. Learn to take authority over your life with God in the driver's seat of your heart.

Words can destroy or create. We have a choice of being constructive with encouraging words or destructive with words of despair. Words have energy and power with the ability to help, heal, hinder, hurt, harm, humiliate and to humble. The Bible says in Proverbs 15:4, "Gentle words bring life and health a deceitful tongue crushes the spirit" and in Proverbs 16:24, "Kind words are like honey sweet to the soul and healthy for the body". Finally, "A person words can be life giving water: words of truth wisdom are a refreshing as a bubbling brook" (Prov.18:4). Further, it states in Matthew, "For by your words you will be justified, and by your words you will be condemned" (Matt.12:37). The power of the word shapes our beliefs, drives our behavior, and ultimately creates our world. When spoken with truth, our words have the ability to change lives. Whether words are written or spoken, they have the power to break and destroy healthy environments as well as relationships. It is vital to always speak truth, but we must be mindful about what we say and how we say it. How we speak is a caution sign for me. Tone arises from our emotional responses when we read, speak or hear the Word. I am focusing on the tone of my words. It is so real to me at this stage of my life -- deliverance in action. Jesus said that His words come directly from God. He said it again and again. Jesus said that His words are spirit and life and that His words will be around for eternity. As I change how I speak about myself and others, I believe this is a mill stone in my journey to elevate myself to the next level of victory in ministry.

FEAR CAN CONTROL YOUR LIFE

You probably do not believe that fear can and will control you in your life, your relationships, and your decision making. For example, there is fear that accompanies obeying the call of God in your life. I remember before I received the chosen call in my life, I was afraid of not understanding. Now I only depend only on the Word. People will derail you and cause you to miss the movement of God in your life. And, if you do not know the source of fear, it is nearly impossible to overcome. In fact, it makes it easy for other people and situations to control you and your actions. Fear is defined as being afraid of something or someone. Fear is a feeling of anxiety and agitation caused by the presence or nearing of danger, evil and pain causing terror, apprehension, dread, timidity and fright. What are the causes of fear -- real or imagined? While there are certain things that trigger fear in most of us, we can learn to become afraid of nearly anything. When we receive the Word, we all have the victory. That is the power of the Word. I believe that Jesus died on the cross for me. I believe in my heart and confess with my mouth. I have received and believe that I have not the spirit of fear.

Fear of failure is greatest of all fears: failure of health, business, finances, love, success etc. There is the fear of the dark, being alone and animals. Some people fear they are misunderstood, while others fear they are losing mental control. Remember, continued and constant fear affects the glands, interferes with digestion and is usually associated nervous symptoms. This will rob the body of divine health and destroy happiness. Medical issues are linked to stress. It is our responsibility to stay healthy to be used by the Kingdom. For the call is real and has responsibility that we alone cannot do; therefore, we need the guidance of the Holy Spirit. Feelings, emotions, and deep affections will always lead us astray without God's word to light our path. The word of God is the only confirmation that we have that we are being led by the Holy Spirit. Think about how our God leads His creation. We must go to the Word in the wilderness. The Bible states "Yahweh went before them by day in pillar of cloud to lead them along the way, and by night in a pillar of fire to give them light" (Exodus 13:21). We all need that light to be led. Even we who are confident in the light of God might sometimes feel it difficult. How do we know when He is leading us? "For all who are being led by the Spirit of God these are sons of God" (Romans 8:14). I pray daily that I am hearing and following the voice of God. Sometimes we are led by our own fleshly impulses. This refers to the battle between flesh and Spirit. The flesh is the opposite of the Holy Spirit. "And I will put my spirit within you, and cause you to walk in my statutes, and ye shall keep my judgments, and do them" (Ezekiel 36:27). The Holy Spirit inspired the scriptures. He leads us into obedience to the scriptures. This is a personal application of the word of God. I believe we are led by revelation inspired in the presence of God that leads us to all truth. I declare now that we will hear our Lord and follow as He has spoken in this season. Hold on to His spoken word for this is the only way to the heart of God. Always focus on your peace. The Word says that in His presence there is a fullness of joy which regulates your peace. "For God hath not given us the spirit of fear; but of power, and of love, and of a sound mind" (2 Tim.1:7). What is a sound mind? The dictionary defines it as the state of a man's mind which is adequate to reason and comes to a judgement upon ordinary subjects, like other rational men. The biblical sober-minded Paul exhorts Timothy to be "sober-minded, endure suffering, do the work of an evangelist, fulfill your ministry" Sober-minded free from intoxicating influences."(Tim.4:5) We do not allow ourselves to be captivated by any type of influence that would lead us away from sound judgment, to. be calm under pressure, self-controlled in all areas, and rational. Paul's instruction to Timothy was to exercise self-control, keep his head and keep a clear mind. See 2 Tim.4:5. Peter warned, "the end of all things is at hand; therefore be self-controlled and sober-minded for the sake of your prayers" (1 Peter 4:7). Those who are sober are alert to the prayers that are needed and tune in to their surroundings. "But fornication, and all uncleanness, or covetous-ness, let it not be once named among you, as becometh saints; Neither filthiness, nor foolish talking, nor jesting, which are not convenient: but rather giving of thanks" (Eph.5:3-4). Being atten-tive to the Word is a wise decision in ministry, only if we want to demonstrate a great impact in the hour of restoration. We the church, in this hour, have been positioned to receive restoration -- receive it now.

Fear is the worst enemy, because you attract what you fear. It is faith turned upside down -- the opposite of faith. "And he saith unto them, why are ye fearful, O ye of little faith? Then he arose and rebuked the winds and the sea; and there was a great calm" (Matthew 8:26). Our confidence must always be in the Word that has been given to us as guidance in our walk with God. We must always trust it by faith to continue to walk in the things of God that has been promised to us.

"If then God so clothe the grass, which is today in the field, and morrow is cast into the oven; how much more will he clothe you, O ye of little faith" (Luke 12:28). Whatever you desire or require is already set before you, you already have what you need. He said before you called, He has already answered. "I call heaven and earth to record this day against life and death, blessing and cursing therefore choose life, that both thou and thy seed may live" (Deut. 30:19). Minister to your family about your Savior that they may know Him. Declare blessing upon your legacy and prepare. **Speak the word of God**. Walk by faith, trusting and believing God's word to return as He has said. His Word will not return void. "So shall my word be that go forth out of my mouth: it shall not return unto me void, but it shall accomplish that which I please, and it shall prosper in the thing whereto I sent it" (Isaiah 55:11). **TRUST THE PROMISE: "GOD IS FAITHFUL, BY WHOM YE WERE CALLED UNTO THE FELLOWSHIP OF HIS SON JESUS CHRIST OUR LORD" (1 Cor.1:9).**

We thank you Lord, Thou wilt shew me the path of life in thy presence is fullness of joy; at Thy right hand there are pleasures for evermore. AMEN

Chaper Four

Broken To Serve

Awaken with the words **broken** to serve you, so humbled in the hand of my Lord. The Lord spoke to me that maintaining relationship with Him had priority in my walk with the Holy Spirit. I am to keep my eyes on the promises. He reminds me of the complete work of the cross, that grace was fully operational in my brokenness. The death of my son left me unable to move forward in my personal life. That I awakened to my environment, the surroundings and conditions of how I got here is so amazing. Paul wrote, "For out of much affliction and anguish of heart I wrote unto you with many tears; not that ye should be grieved, but that ye might know the love which I have more abundantly unto you" (2 Cor. 2:4). Yes, as I find myself in the hands of my Lord, He is bringing me to the awareness of who I am in Him. I must awaken from the place of indecision and wait for that soft still voice that sometimes is so soft that I can hardly hear it; but through His word I know He is speaking. Then we say yes Lord, even though the environment might be hostile. When we are called by God there must be a testing of our faith. Our faith must be tested as broken bread and poured out wine, all for the glory of

God. Faith is when you can't see or know, but you trust His word to manifest that for which you have prayed and hoped. "I am more than, Nay in all these things we are more than conquerors through him that loved us" (Rom 8:37). Surely with all my heart I thank Him for loving us. "Do I love me?" is the question at this time in my life. We must always say what He is saying about us -- yes Lord, I repeat your words I love what you are doing in my life. In my youth, I did not really know how important it was to continue to love myself. But when a person finds him/herself in sinking sand, thinking there is no way out, God, who is rich in glory through Christ, has His hand on that person. He was there all the time. We have had the wonderful opportunity to deliver many from hurt and pain from their past defeats. At this moment we are generating the love of God throughout our hearts and know that He is our Lord and we are totally yielded at every second. I think of the love that the Father bestowed upon us when He sent His only Son Jesus Christ to die on the cross for our sins. "For God so loved the world, that he gave his only begotten Son, that whosoever believeth in him should not perish, but have everlasting life" (John 3:16). Today I am adding to my teaching the strong desire to make sure my ministry always stays true to the Word. So, studying the Word has moved to the top of my list to instruct my mentees and my congregation as well. The power of His word comes to my mind sitting in His presence, meditating on His love. Words have energy. We are the ones who must make a quality decision what that energy will be. We must always trust His word by faith, the key to carry in your heart and mouth. Out of the abundance of heart the mouth will speak. Truly it is important that we turn this pain into power and be overcomers to express a wonderful testimony birth for our King. Then we shall shine forward in His Kingdom. "That he would grant you, according to the riches not my mine His riches, of His glory to be strengthened with might by His Spirit in the inner man" (Eph. 3:16). I do not have to depend on my knowledge or my thinking because He has me in His hand. I trust His words to frame my world; not I, but the Christ that lives in me propels me out of defeat. When I find myself only in His presence there is peace, joy and total victory in every area of my life. What can I say to these things that the Lord has placed in my heart? Yes, I will obey and do the work because after the brokenness comes victory. We are sometimes broken to serve. With Christ all things are possible. "But Jesus beheld them and said unto them with men this is impossible but with God all things are possible" (Mt. 19:26).

What do you do when you are called to do a work as a female? I was told I was not good enough, that God couldn't use me in His work in His Kingdom -- no not a female. As we reflect on His words – He is in control. I can do all things through Christ who has strengthened me in my brokenness. I totally yield to the testing of my faith in a strange world. With my enemies on every side, I was in a hostile environment. Those around me doubted my call from God and as an RN at the bedside of hurting people.I worked 2 jobs in ICU/OPEN HEART UNIT /CCU. As an agency nurse, the staff noted that when I was taking care of a patient, their recovery was excellent. I remember this case vividly. Working at Missouri Baptist hospital, I was assigned this university student that had a stroke while at school. Her case was touch and go, meaning she was in a critical state. As I was taking care of her I had an encounter with my Holy Spirit. I was propelled to pray while working and singing in the Spirit. He would lead me and I yielded to my environment that was set by the Spirit of God. The young student began to improve quickly. I reported in her chart and notified the neurologist of her condition. He was so shocked that he came back to the hospital in the middle of the night. I worked the midnight shift as my second job (11P-7A nursing) -- again I said yes. The doctor needed to check her vitals and see if this was real because I was reporting a miracle. Her mother was in and out of the waiting room and was amazed by her quick recovery, needless to say. I gave my awesome God all the Glory. I rose from a broken young woman that He had called to be a nurse in December 1977. This was after dropping out of high school to marry my first love Mr. Martin Olden Lewis Jr. at the young age of 17 years old. He was my best friend. As I call his name now, I remember our young, everlasting love. I could have placed it in a bottle with a cap and held it tight as not to spill a drop. I did not want to waste this precious love. Today, I am able to allow that unconditional love to equip me. I continue to love God's people unconditionally through ministry, helping many young millennial men and women that are sent to me by my loving and caring Creator God. In my youth, I was focused on my sons and my grandsons. I wanted them to be great men with purpose. That is what my heart wanted for them. But, we must always trust the process, it may take a while; but they well make it with the help of our Creator. I declare that the blood of Jesus will cover our children through the process of growing to be great men of God. We, as leaders, are called by God and must be in the work to mentor and hold up our young people in prayer. Their is no greater gift than unconditional love which will never give up.

WITH LOVE EVERY ENCOUNTER THERE IS A MOVE OF GOD

Loving God's people is a gift from Him. "Charity suffer long, and kind; charity envy not; (resentful longing aroused by someone else's possessions qualities, or luck) charity vaunt not itself, is not puffed up, Do not behave itself unseemly, seek not her own, is not easily provoked, thinketh no evil" (1 Cor 13:4-5). Our God is love and the fire in our hearts for Him is revealed when we allow Him to use us in His love expressed unconditionally. This love is without conditions or limits. It is straight from the throne room of God and strengthened through test and trials in life experiences. Can you care without getting instant feed-back? We trust the process and believe that the church is in the season of restoration. So much pain has come from our government being in a dysfunctional state for four years. First the church then the dysfunctional world needs restoration. We believe healing will come through the Word of God. If you have the ability and the authority, you can catch the wind of the Spirit, which is ordained by our Creator who has ordered our steps. The steps of good man are ordered by the Lord. "The steps of A good man are ordered by the Lord and he delight in his way" (Ps. 37:23). Our Lord is raising up leaders with voices that speak the Word of God with power and demonstration. "He that has an ear, let him hear what the spirit saith unto the church" (Rev 2:11). We believe that there is raising awareness of the true prophets to come forward. At all cost seek the voice of God in this season. We can't depend on another to lead us in this season. Seek ye the Kingdom. "But seek ye first the kingdom of God, and his righteousness; and all these things shall be added unto you" (Mt. 6:33). Lord, we thank you for guidance in this end time season of restoration; in You we live and move and have our being. With restoration their must always be love at the foundation, then truth. We can depend on what is being spoken so that we may receive the revelation from heaven. Then, we can walk in the full manifestation of deliverance revealed in Him with love as the foundation Our Father God.

At Immanuel Temple - God with Us, we use a tool called a Prayer Guide For Deliverance Step by Step. We were trained with this technique from a teaching guide in 2009. Many have been delivered using this tool in a private setting.

Step 1: **Pray** for the Holy Spirit to guide –name—to the truth. Pray that they would know the truth and the truth would set them free.

Step 2: **Understand** Truth vs. lies and deceptions.

Help the person you are ministering to get the understanding of truth vs lies and deceptions. To begin with, explain to them Jesus said that understanding the truth sets us free. See John 8:31-32. If understanding the truth sets us free then it must be a lie or deception that keeps us in bondage, A lie or deception is a wrong belief or understanding that we hold that is contrary to the Word of God (truth). Jesus said that the devil is the father of all lies in John 8:43-44, and that the devil comes to steal and kill and destroy but Jesus came to give us abundant life (John 10:10).

Step 3: **Identify** Negative Emotion.

Have the person go to the most recent situation where they felt negative emotions.

Step 4: **Identify** the Lie.

Step 5: **Help** them Understand What They Believe Is A Lie.

Step 6: **Establish** Their Will to Be Free.

Step 7: **Explain** Prayer Process.

Ministry of the Holy Spirit.

Step 8: **Understand** Our Authority as A Believer.

Take authority over the kingdom of darkness and the strong man guarding the stronghold of lies in the person's belief system (Luke11:17-22).

Step 9: **Finding** Root Memory.

Say repeat after me...

Holy Spirit take me back to the root memory where I learned the lie that says___ Ask them___.

What memory is the Holy Spirit showing you and how old you are in the memory?

BARRIERS TO CHILDHOO ROOT MEMORIES

1) Demonic oppression
2) Unforgiveness
3) Unconfessed sin
4) Vows
5) Traumatic experience such as accident, grief or rape

Using discernment decides if you should work through any barriers, as needed.

Step 10: **Invite** Jesus Into Memory and Establish Truth.

Step 11: **Pray** through Deliverance

Step 12: **Confirm** Freedom

Visit root memory and check the heart. They should no longer feel the heart tension but should have a sense of peace. Go to recent experience and check heart.

Step 13: What to Expect

We really need to prepare people for the fact that their new-found belief will be tested.

Step 14: **Meditation**

"When the unclean spirit goes out of a man, he walketh through dry places, seeking rest and finding none. Then he sayeth, I will return into my house from whence I came out, and when he is come, he findeth it empty. Swept and garnished. Then goeth he and take him seven other spirits more wicked than himself, and they enter in and dwell there; and the last state of the man is worse than the first. Even so shall it be unto this wicked generation." (Mt 12:43-45).

Place A Blessing on Their lives

HEVENLY Father in the mighty name of Jesus Christ, I declare, Blessings upon , NAME___

And ask the Holy Spirit to establish them in this truth, as If they have never believed the lie.

Holy Spirit, mature them, Spirit, Soul and Body, and establish them to their maturity, so their life is the way it would be if they always had believed the Truth.

Heavenly Father, we ask that everything this lie has stolen be restored to them, now. Every relationship, possession and wholeness in every area in their life is returned to them, as if the lie had never planted in their heart. (Name)___ I bless you with and declare that your days under bondage of this lie is over, in Jesus Name we both agree and say, Amen.

Chapter Five

Every Idle Word /Power Of
Your Words

"**B**ut I say unto you, That every idle word that men shall speak, they shall give account thereof in the day of judge" (Matt.12:36). Idle words are those words of expression from the heart that seek for sinful pleasure without the obligation of action. Example: dirty jokes, foolish talking and with empty words very careless words. The Greek phrase is rem argos, meaning careless or inactive or unprofitable words. Jesus is stating in contrast as idle can mean spending time doing nothing-- empty words. Words are very powerful. In Genesis 1, God's words are so powerful that as He spoke they created everything. But even humanity can do powerful things as we speak the words of God. Using our words we can create, as Solomon wrote in Proverb 18:21, death and life can be seen in life situations. In court rooms, witnesses (right or wrong) can determine a man's destiny. Even the power of words can be encouraging and give hope, or words can defeat or discourage, destroying a whole life. Jesus is contrasting the good person with the evil things in the heart of an evil person. We are admonished to make the best use of our words, what is in our heart. "You brood of vipers, How can you speak good, when you are evil? For out of the abundance the heart the mouth speaks" (Matt. 12:34). "Do not let any unwholesome talk come out of your mouths, but only what is helpful for building us up according to their needs that it may benefit those who listen" (Eph. 4:29). In the Bible, James advises us how hard it is to control the tongue: "No human being can tame the tongue it is a restless evil, full of deadly poison" (Jame.3:8). Further he says "...brothers and sisters, do not slander one another. Anyone who speaks against a brother or sister or judges them speaks against the law and judge sit. When you judge the law, you are not keeping it, but sitting in judgement on it There is only one Lawgiver and Judge, the one who able to save and destroy" (James 4:11-12). There is a weighty consequences of our words even our careless words. We must learn to yield our body's members, including our tongue, to the control of the Holy Spirit, the only one who can tame the tongue. "Set a guard over my mouth Lord Now in Jesus Name keep watch over the door of my lips" (Ps.141:3).

VENTING: HOW TO AND WHY

Venting is the term used to describe allowing strong emotion over a specific situation. The expression or release of energy gives free expression to a strong emotion.

When we speak out at length toward our spouses or close friends about what just happened or how our boss mistreated us, we are venting. The term venting comes from the idea of providing an outlet for air, liquid or steam. An example of things we vent are air conditioners, clothes, dryers and pressure cookers. When we express our strong emotions through words, writings or physical aggression, we are venting our emotions. Venting can be a harmless way to process built up passions over an event or conversation. Venting can allow us to calm down and return to thinking rational. As long as our venting does not take a sinful form involving foolish language, hateful speech or physical harm, it can be a healthy way to calm ourselves. Venting is best done with a trusted person that is not connected to the event or emotion, and will not hold us responsible for everything we say in those heated moments. See Proverbs 18:24. Likewise, we should be willing to allow friends to vent to us when needed. We need to maintain the word in our heart and to keep focus while venting. "And I tell this you must give an account on judgement day for every idle word you speak" (Matt 12:36). In this quote, Jesus warns us that God keeps record of our words. What we speak matters to Him. Venting does not give us the right to disobey the Lord with our words. Rambling is confusing, rehashing the event over and over again, or even refusing to forgive and move on is one way we speak idle words. When venting becomes our way of dealing with issues or our pass-time, we may have crossed a line from temporary release to permanent lifestyle.We must gain self-control in our walk with God. "Do not let any unwholesome talk come out of your mouth, but only what is helpful for building others up according to their needs, that it may benefit those who listen" (Eph. 4:29). Venting over and over to release an ugly heart will not allow the Lord to change us. Do not use foul language to curse people and house hateful thoughts. When venting, we are to remain self-controlled and not assume that injustice gives us permission to contaminate our mouths with unwholesome talk.AND "DON'T SIN BY LETTING ANGER CONTROL YOU.' Don't let the sun go down while you are still angry (NLT Eph.4:26) In your anger we can destroy families, relationship and lives, sometimes suppressed anger can do much destruction. Never give place to the devil. (Eph.4:27kj) Venting is one way we can quickly process our anger and release it before nightfall. When we keep frustration bottled up, we run the risk of physical ailments, anxiety, insomnia, and other medical issues. Venting is a safe way to handle emotions that are too explosive to keep inside our heads. This verse warns us that if we do not quickly find healthy outlets for our anger, we allow the devil to step in and bring more harm. When we vent our frustration in healthy ways, we can also bring good out of something bad. Literature, art and music are ways to vent that can lead to beauty, wisdom and worship. I use music to keep calm. I have listened to the artist Ben Tankard since 1993 and I have been listening to gospel jazz which helps me walk through many challenges on my journey.

Victory and achievements, desires met, dreams fulfilled -- we can create a world in our imagination where everything is right and all of our desires are met. "Blessed are those who hunger and thirst for righteousness, for they shall be satisfied" (Matt.5:6). But are these desires and spoken words coming from the well of God in our lives for His divine plan? Jesus promises satisfaction to those who are hungry and thirsty for righteousness. What words are coming out of our mouths when we don't get what we think we deserve, when people don't say what we want them to say. How do we treat people when they don't do what we want? Are we displaying the kind of character that shows obedience to God? If so, He can depend on us to build His Kingdom on earth.

BUILDING CHARACTER:

Every word of God proves true. He defends all who come to Him for protection (Prov.30:5). He will always call on us to speak TRUTH. His prophetic voice is protected throughout the earth. Walking in truth is the pathway to build character and to work on your personality, such your behavior or attitude. To make ourselves better people, we should learn from our mistakes which builds character. The things that will build our character, such as humility, is the beginning of wisdom. We must be open to new ways of living out our principles and values. Whether it is to love others, or doing the right thing will make our character more steadfast. Be intentional. Integrity does not happen by accident. We are all products of our thoughts and habits. Be intentional about filling your thoughts with good things. Practice self-discipline on purpose. High expectation is a must. Surround yourself with people who have high expectations. Be responsible for yourself first. Similar to when you are on alert in a plane, follow the flight attendants instructions and place your mask on first. Then you can help someone else. Lose the pride or never let it develop. Open yourself up to accountability. Let others push you up to higher character. Continue to improve and trust the process. Remember that lack of trust is our biggest expense and remember the **very thing of value is built on trust**. Be accountable for your actions. We all must be accountable in order to build character. Building character is no simple task. We must work hard (on purpose) to build and maintain good character.

"For all God's words are right, and everything he does is worthy of our trust" (Ps.33:4). Be mindful of words we are speaking and have spoken. Slow to speak quick to hear. "Wherefore, my beloved brethren, let every man be swift to hear, slow to speak, slow to wrath" (Jam.1:19). This verse is telling us to wait before speaking which can prevent trauma and allow us time to develop wisdom and Godly character.

"For the Lord grants wisdom! His every word is a treasure of knowledge and understanding" (Prov.2:6). Studying the word of God will bring soundness of an action or decision. When we apply good judgement, we grow in the proper use of words for God's kingdom. Our words should demonstrate good judgement and the quality of being wise. Think before you speak -- slow down wait and listen.

"Also is my word. I send it out, and It shall accomplish all I want it to and prosper everything I send it. You will live in joy and peace the mountain and hills, the trees of the field all the world around you will rejoice" (Isa. 55:11-12). Always remember, we can't always retrieve our words. Once spoken they are hanging out in the atmosphere. I remember so many times in a group setting, I spoke words that I regretted and wanted to erase them. My Lord how powerful are our words. I am learning and thanking you for allowing me to study such a power awareness of our words.

"But he answered and said, it is written, Man shall not live by bread alone, but by every word that proceedeth out of the mouth of God" (Matt.4:4). Jesus knew the Word and it was now in His mouth. Giving Him victory over the devil at a time of temptation, we need to study and trust the words that we speak while having faith to know that His word is true.

"And Jesus answered him, saying, It is written, that man shall not live by bread alone, but by every word of God" (Luke 4:4). Jesus' new Bread is a means to an end; but also the Word is eternal food. Bread alone in not complete man, we need provision for eternal bread. Bread is a physical provision, but the Word is spiritual eternal supply never ending.

"Neither filthiness, nor foolish talking, nor jesting, which are not convenient: but rather giving of thanks" (Eph.5:4). In other words, don't speak according to the world; but rather the Holy Spirit, who gives us what to say and the principles of the Lord Jesus the Christ, the Son of the living God.

"I have sworn by myself. The word is gone out of my mouth in righteousness, and shall not return, That unto me every knee shall bow, every tongue shall swear" (Isa.45:23). God is faithful and always true to His word. There is a commandment that we must revere our creator God with obedience by faith to partake in the deliverance and complete work of the cross. How dependable is your word? Can people trust your word? Now is time for all of us to evaluate our words and make a quality decision to make changes as needed.

A DECREE UNTO GOD:

Now we declare Victory in the area of our lives. Yes, we are trying to stay in good standing with our Creator needing to be in His presence that He may manifest His glory in our lives. We praise You for healing and deliverance for us first, then those that He sends. In the mighty Name of Jesus Christ the Son of the living God our Creator.

Chapter Six

The Glory Of God

WALK WITH ME

In John 3, there was a man of Pharisees, a ruler of the Jews: "...
the same came to Jesus by night, and said unto him, 'Rabbi,
we know that thou art a teacher come from God: for no man can
do these miracles that thou do, except God be with him.' Jesus
answered and said unto him, 'Verily, verily I say unto thee, Except
a man be born again, he cannot see the Kingdom of God.'" (John
3:1-3). "That which is born of the flesh is flesh; and that which is
born of the Spirit is spirit. Ye must be born again" (John 3:6-7).
"Jesus said Verily, verily, I say unto thee, We speak that we do know,
and testify that we have seen; and ye receive not our witness. If I
told you earthly things, and ye believe not, how shall ye believe, if
I tell you of heavenly things" (John 3:11-12). This chapter details
how Jesus came into the world so that mankind would know the
nature and character of God and our Spiritual rebirth from heaven.
Nicodemus came at night and questioned Him, because he knew
that Jesus did not perform these signs without God. His decision

to meet with Jesus, along with his position as ruler of the Jews, may be linked. Jesus was not a popular man with Jewish leaders. He was usually talked about in a negative view. Nicodemus recognized a more positive side of Jesus and His relationship to God. Rather than approaching Jesus during the day, his timing may reflect a fear of being seen with Jesus. Night is a symbol of evil and sin, but Jesus explained more fully that a man must be born of water and of the Spirit. Water is a symbol for the Wisdom of God. Faith comes by hearing God's words of wisdom. We are cleansed and birthed by the Words. Wisdom is poured forth like water from the fountain of the Word. Then a wise man's knowledge wells up in a flood, and his spirit as a counsel like a fountain of life. "With salvation a person's words can be life-giving water; words of true wisdom are as refreshing as a bubbling brook" (Pro.18:4). "With joy we shall draw water from the well of salvation" (Is.12:3). Jesus explains that God is Spirit. Once we hear the words of the Father and we repent, we are cleansed by the blood of Jesus. Then our bodies become a vessel ready for the presence making us Spirit born. The wind and the spirit are one same as 'pneuma' -- flesh is flesh. The Father breathes and His breath carries His words and those who hear and obey them, become Spirit born. The Spirit of Wisdom flows where it wants, and we are hearing Its voice right this minute; but we are unaware from where the voice comes or to where it returns. Nicodemus was astonished and asked how can this be possible? Jesus uses three words from above and again, "hypsoo", meaning lift up and exalt and "pneuma", meaning wind and spirit. It is very important for the reader to understand the nature of this conversation between these two. Recognize the human ignorance by Nicodemus that actually kept him from seeing and believing. Jesus knows exactly what he is doing, and He is making all efforts to bring Nicodemus to a right understanding of who He is and who God is and how the new covenant relationship works. We in humanity must not allow our intellect, the faculty of reasoning, and our objective approach to reject the word of God. Then for sure we may sound like Nicodemus. Let's all receive the Word in our hearts and allow the wisdom of His word to bring us to a place to receive His spirit and become born again. We should build the kingdom of God with fear and trembling, not touching His glory on our journey until Jesus reappears. I am sending an invitation to all who accept to come and walk with me on our new awakening journey.

When the Almighty called me to pastor, the first thing He did was give me a tree to build the foundation of His kingdom with Jesus as the root. He led me to study in the Tabernacle of God. Truly this has been an ongoing teaching in our ministry. I have used this prayer throughout our ministry. Being in God's presence has sustained me, with so many words spoken out of context, being different and not a standard church. Those words were surely not from God. Absolutely we continue to serve God's people even in a pandemic. We have served with excellence because of His manifested presence - His Shekinah presence. Now we sit at the computer writing about this wonderful journey, the radiance and splendor of His Glory. We walk and teach about the high standard of holiness.

My eyes have seen the radiance of the Lord -- that means the law in action. We cannot see God. God is principle --first in order of importance (main). Power is the Supreme Intelligence within us; and what we have and continue to see is the proof of God Himself. "...Prove Thou me herewith, said the Lord of Hosts, if I will open the windows of (heaven) and pour you out a blessing, so great, there be not room enough to receive it." (Mal. 3:10). We prove God with our obedience (submission to another's authority trusting in Him to do the work. "Everyone must submit himself to the governing authorities, for there is no authority except that which God has established" (Romans 13:1). "I exhort therefore, that first all supplication, prayers, intercessions, and giving of thanks, be made for all men: For kings and for all that are in authority; that we may lead a quiet and peaceable life in all godliness and honesty" (1Tim2:1-2). Entering into His courts with praise and thanksgiving we present our bodies a living sacrifice unto the Lord. Living in that place of submission is surely our keeping power. We sit here with the breath of life flowing through our heart, knowing that this breath comes with new life in Him.

MY TESTIMONEY UNTO HIM

For months I had been short of breath and was taking an inhaler prescribed by the respiratory doctor. I was getting worse taking this inhaler for over a year or more so he increased my dosage, sad but true. He did this even after I told him not to, this was a set up from the enemy. I knew this was not my Lord. I really was tired and unable to clean my house. Yes, that was a hard pill to swallow, short of breath and an elevated heart rate. My body was experiencing respiratory failure, the reverse of what the medication was prescribed to do. I sought my Lord and He instructed me to stop using the inhaler and go back to my essential oils. My faith had to rise above my nursing knowledge. The almighty Father was flowing with me. I continued to speak the creative words of healing all day as it would come into my heart. I said I obeyed, now I am healed. Glory! He has performed a miracle and my health became stronger daily. I give Him all the praise and glory for excellent health. By His stripes I am healed in the mighty name of Jesus Christ. "Who his own self bare our sins in his own body on the tree, that we, being dead to sins, should live unto righteousness: by whose stripes ye were healed" (1 Pet. 2:24). The spoken word continues to have power in His name and we give Him praise for all, allow His praises to be in my mouth.

WALKING IN WISDOM AND CREATIVE INSIGHT-POWER

Power is the capacity or ability to direct or influence the behavior of others or the course of events. It is the ability to do something or act in a particular way, especially as a faculty or quality (the power of speech). For me, since studying the spoken word and its power, I am very conscience of my tone and it has been a blessing for me today. In the Bible, power has a deeper meaning as a description of strength of mind, moral qualities of a person, and power of his/her faith, etc. It means that a person that does not depend on outward things. In whatever we face, we cannot allow our circumstances to stop our power within to hold on the promises of God. The full meaning of power is the ability to do or act; the capability of doing or accomplishing something; strength; might; force; and the possession of control or command over people. The authority of words have tremendous power over our minds. Power comes from a Latin word "potere", which means to be able; but things with power are much more able to exert a lot of force. The powers that be are those who hold authority, and the power behind the throne refers to people who exert influence without being formally in charge. It is the possession of control and influence (the power of his love saved her). Someone with power has physical strength or they're in control of things. A weakling who's in charge of a business still has a lot of power. Influence is power. We release our soul, mind, will, emotions and flesh unto our Lord who has power within to keep us in His perfect peace in the mist of anything that we are facing in our Lord Jesus Christ.

At our church, we had a minister and his wife moon-lighting at our ministry. His wife was not ready to join, they were coming for months; but I noticed that he was always in the hospital every week on ventilators. It was a serious condition. As I was praying, the Holy Spirit instructed me to tell his wife that he was walking in and out of Glory, and they needed to make a true commitment to God. Bless be unto our God -- after they joined, it had been several months since he had to go back in the hospital. His condition and his stress level is down they are both doing well. He testifies about his healing, no more trips to the hospital; whereas he used to go every week. We thank you Lord and we give you praise and glory for your promises. Amen

Do you know we are made for God's glory? His glory is a gift to us, His creation. This is our inheritance given to all God's children. When we are invited to into God's presence, we dwell in His glory. In that presence we receive His love, grace, understanding of His will and His heart toward us. This is where we experience God's divine power towards us. In this place, His power transforms our lives revealing His majesty, His weighty glory with healing, saving and deliverance -- power manifested. Sorry to say many Christians are not aware of this truth and are not living in the glory of God. They are settling for less in this manifested relationship that is available daily, hourly and every second of our walk with Him. The essence of His glory is revealed in us as we yield to His kingdom. Do not resist Him by walking in pride, doubt and unbelief that His Shekinah presence is not real. Our God is everywhere, surely; but He does not manifest His presence everywhere. Let's explain this statement. God has many facets of His nature and character. There are numerous features of God's glory that are revealed. He desires to show the dimensions of His glory on earth today as we, His creation, live and serve Him. It is true God is omnipresent-everywhere at once.

He has laws in place to follow so we will experience His greatness.

WHERE HE IS WORSHIPPED IN SPIRIT AND IN HIS TRUTH

WHERE HE IS CONTINUALLY HONORED AND REVEALED

Old Testament believers saw the glory of God manifested among Hebrew people -- His chosen. In the New Testament, we see His glory manifested among the Jewish and the Gentile believers. In His Son, Jesus, God's people saw forms of a cloud known as the shekinah, a Hebrew word referring to" dwelling place of God" or "the place God rests". The presence of God surpass the spiritual realm and manifests itself into the physical world in which we believers live. This is where He allow us to know Him in His activity of His splendor now. He is working in our lives where His power is manifested. Shekinah is the immediate and intimate activity of God. It is His glory described, which is the essence, nature, attributes and perfection of His character and personality. Shekinah glory is the visible manifestation of His presence to mankind

EXAMPLES OF HIS SHEKINAH

I went to Azusa Conference in Tulsa Oklahoma in the early nineties where I saw the cloud of His glory for the first time. It was an awesome, brilliant and illuminated scene. This was the first place I heard people of God singing in the Spirit. Every year until the conference was cancelled, I was compelled to go yearly in April, just to experience His presence. I could feel His presence when we arrived at the airport. Glory to His name as we remember the great moments of being in this environment for that season. Bishop Pearson's church and ministries would start by fasting in January, preparing for our arrival from all over the

world. I met so many great people, and received so many impartations from the greatness of God. As we write, we pray for Apostle
Carlton Pearson and his family. When our fellowship was at 120
N. Cardinal Place, Christopher and Travis were practicing on the
keyboard in my office. Christopher showed up in front of the staff
with a radiate glory over his face. He pointed back to the sanctuary
we all ran and saw Travis' hands moving. He was playing glorious
sounds from heaven. Travis continued to play with Chris for our
church for years, increasing that glory in our sanctuary. There he
learned to create glory with those keys. I continue to give God
praise for the young men. They are still in my life. God continues
to send others to experience the manifested presence of His great
power in an earthy vessel. How wonderful is our awesome God.
He uses His broken vessels to bring life so amazing. I thank the
Lord for His Manifested Glory in our assembly of worship.

His essence is His total sum -- His character, attributes and
virtues. It is the brilliance of who He is. His majesty is the highest
level of exaltation. The Messiah's royalty and splendor is available.
It is the very essence of His glory.

We must create an atmosphere of the heavenly, meaning the
sound and rhythms, the strong, regular, repeated patterns of
movement or sound. These are the instruction I received from my
God in prayer years ago. I am compelled to follow and it's working.
I receive healing daily, giving glory to His wonderful name -- Jesus.
We found the sound for worship at Immanuel Temple -- God with
us sanctuary. Experiencing the movement of God at every service,
no one left the way they arrived.

In the glory of God every need is met. To really have a fulfilled
life, we must remain connected to God's presence. Our breath
is given in His presence. God created the first man, Adam, out
of the dust of the earth. He gave him His breath of life. As is
recounted in Genesis, the Lord God formed man of the dust of the
ground and breathed into his nostrils the breath of life; and man

became a living being. Being an RN, we were taught the value of life. We first check for breathing and if we found a patient down or non-responsive, we start CPR. Life is in our breath, without it we become brain dead. At creation we had no sickness, poverty or death. Humanity had abundant life. Man was in the presence of God before the fall; therefore, when we are in the presence of God we are restored back to redemption. There is no sickness, poverty or death. Creative miracles abound. Before the fall, humanity had no knowledge of sickness, pain and sorrow because humanity was with God.

The presence of God is an atmosphere prepared by Him. Before God began to create anything, He first made ready the environment that sustained His creation. Before creation of humanity, He created provision to sustain man. (Genesis 1:9-25) states that the oceans and the rivers were created for fish and other living things. God created the firmament of heavens, and then He created the stars and planets that function per His design for His will.

He created the garden of Eden and God put man in the garden in His presence and glory. What does Eden mean? It means pleasure or delight. Garden means an enclosure or a fence. When we are in His glory, we are in His protective environment. Sin caused man to fall short of the glory of God, and to be exiled from His presence. "For all have sinned and fall short of the glory of God" (Rom. 3:23). This means our sins must be forgiven prior to humanity attempting to get in the presence of God. Repentance means sincere regret or remorse. It is a must in order to stand in God's presence. God's presence is pure and uncontaminated. Thank God for His plain of restoration. "The Lord said longsuffering to us-ward, not willing that any should perish, but that all should come to repentance" (2 Peter 3:9). His plan for redemption is sending His Son, Jesus, to the earth to be born of a virgin, walk as an earthly vessel and lead a sinless life. Jesus died to atone for our sins. Jesus was raised from death to life ascending to heaven with the shedding of His blood. Jesus redeemed us to eternal life, that is being back into righteousness or right standing with God. When we are restored, we received the power of the Holy Spirit. God has given us the power to live a life of holiness, to maintain the redemptive plan of our God. The glory of God is present at the time of salvation; but we as believers must by faith believe we can obtain the redemptive work of the cross which restores all that was lost at Eden in the presence of God. We are carriers of the presence of God with His indwelling Holy Spirit. Jesus said "I am the way, the truth, and life" (John 14:6). When we stay connected to our true environment, we will walk in true life in His presence. "He who abides in Me, and I in Him, bears much fruit; for without me, you can do nothing' (John 15:5). We are made for God's glory. We must actively seek God and His glory through praise, worship and being totally surrendered to His divine will. Remember what the Word says, "..the Spirit indeed is willing, but the flesh is weak" (Matt.26:41). We believe from this inspired scripture that we were on the mind of our Creator. In the beginning of my pastoring, He compelled me to study the Tabernacle of God, to save my life from destruction, after the death of my precious son, Apostle Maurice Olden Lewis. I was weak in my soul and my heart was broken; but I continued preaching, serving God's people. I held on as my Lord had given me those words in 1992, when my journey began in ministry. I had "HOLD-ON" as my license plate until 1999 after the death of Ben D. Byas, my second husband. Two years later I was called pastor. Glory to His divine protection, covering me in my obedience to the call and the grace to follow. Now walking into my twentieth year ready to run this ordained race, I have attached the study of the tabernacle of God I declare , "enjoy your journey that has been set before you this day as you study the shadow of Jesus." **Now we will continue to give Him glory and honor in the mighty name of Jesus Christ our Lord and Savior. Let us** now enter His courts with praise and thanksgiving. Posturing ourselves to receive from Him.

WORSHIP
STEPS TO WORSHIPPING GOD IN HIS TABERNACLE

THE SHADOW OF JESUS

1. ENTER THE TABERNACLE **COURT** (EX. 27:9; 40:38). As you walk from your family tent, you can see the cloud of God's presence over the tabernacle (dwelling place). You draw near filled with fire, smoke, bleating animals, bustling workers. and Tabernacle. Enter in with praise thanking God for the blood of Jesus. **God could only be approached with repentance and sacrifice. We enter into his courts with praise and thanksgiving the fruit of your lips that openly profess his name even in the darkest of times we can praise God for His love, his sovereignty, and His promise to be near us when we call (Ps. 145:18).**

2. SACRIFICE AT THE **BRONZEN ALTER** (Ex.27:1-8; Lev. 1:1-4). If your sacrifice is approved, Sin was serious. **Only shed blood**, which stands for life could pay for sin. Here we present our body a living sacrifice unto God. **Repentance.**

3. SUBMIT to the priest Jesus who laid His blood at the alter when He died on the cross. His blood paid the penalty for sin. He is our High Priest today. Alter meaning high priest.

4. WASH AT THE **BRONZEN LAVEN** (Ex.30:17-21; 38:8). This is a large shallow basin of water, holiness, gleaming as brightly as a mirror. The priest washed his hands before

and after the sacrifice. Here the washing of word we see ourselves in the mirror of the word. (John 15:3; 17:17)

THE HOLY PLACE

5. **GOLDEN LAMPSTAND**/CHRIST/HOLY SPIRIT ENTERING THE **HOLY PLACE. The light stood for God's presence** (Ex.25:23-26; 37). No windows and seven golden candlelight lampstands stood for God's presence. Christ is the light of the world. The Holy Spirit is the oil providing the shining forward in a dark world releasing the seven spirits of God. The priest and High priest are in charge of keeping oil in the lamp stands. Jesus is our High priest in the New Testament. "And the Spirit of the Lord shall rest upon him, the spirit of wisdom and understanding, the spirit of counsel and might, the spirit of knowledge and of the fear of the Lord" (Isa. 11:1-2). Finally, He reveals the knowledge of Christ (John 15:26; 16:15) and produces in us a reverential respect for God. Here is where we acknowledge the Holy Spirit and His gifts revealed in our hearts.

5b. **TABLE OF SHOWBREAD**. Remain in the holy place where the light shines upon the word of God as we partake of the bread at the table 6. Loaves side by side totaling twelve which means authority in the word of God when spoken in the presence of God. The bread, given weekly, showed thankfulness for His provision, and the joy of fellowship at the table with Him. Here we speak the word over our Life and Ministry.

THE ALTAR OF INCENSE (Ex.30:1-10;34-38) is the place for **intercessory prayer -- the incense stood for**

constant prayer. Jesus our High Priest intercedes for us in heaven at the right hand of the Father. We acknowledge Christ's blood which gives value to our prayers before God (Heb 9:14; 12:24) and pray for our family as we are directed by the Holy Spirit. Jesus asked the father protection from the world **Jesus is our Intercessor.** Heb. 7:25; Rom.8:34; John17:1-26. Jesus is our Mediator. Heb. 8:6 9:15;1TIM.2:5. The Holy Spirit (Confronter). John 14:16; 15:26; 16:7. Intercedes for us Rom. 8:26, 27

6. **THE VEIL** TO SEPARATE A BARRIER BETWEEN GOD AND MAN, shutting God in and man out (Lev.16:2) and the curtain permitted access to worship after the priest had met the required conditions set forth in the Mosaic law. This curtain was ripped from top to bottom when our savior Jesus died on the cross to give us access to enter into the presence of God. Prior to that, sin had separated us from God.

THE MOST HOLY PLACE

THE ARK OF THE COVENANT AND THE MERCY SEAT (Ex.25:10-22; 37:1-9). In the spirit of reverence -- in the Old Testament only the high priest could enter the holy of holies. He offered mercy so sinful people could approach Him. Jesus became the High priest (Heb.4:14-16). Now we can enter into the presence. The Ark = testimony (Ex.25:22). In the ark there were three items: the golden pot had manna; Aaron's rod that budded; and the ten commandments. The Ark's contents showed His desire to teach, provide and dwell among us. In the (covenant) Mercy Seat (Ex.25:17-22; 37:6-9) blood was sprinkled several times in the tabernacle. Before the mercy seat in the holies of holies, blood was sprinkled in same manner as the blood of the bullock (Lev.16:15) Second, he sprinkled the horns of the altar of incense seven times to cleanse it from the contamination of Israel (Ex.30:10). Third, he went to brazen altar and mixed the blood of the bullock and goat in one basin. He dipped his finger and sprinkled it on the horns of brazen altar seven times (Lev.16:19) for uncleanness of Israel. They waited patiently and prayerful outside of the tabernacle for the high priest to appear before them. We, New Testament believers, no longer need a priest to tell us our sins are forgiven. We have the blood of Jesus and our confession along with our holy life to receive the promises in His presence. **GLORY IS REVEALED AND THE VOICE OF GOD SPEAKS IN THIS PLACE OF GLORY -- THE SHEKINAH** (THE GLORY OF DIVINE PRESENCE, CONVENTIONALLY REPRESENTED AS LIGHT OR INTERPRETED SYMBOLICALLY).

"For the of the flesh is in the blood;
and I have given it to you upon the altar.
To make an atonement for your souls;
for it is the blood that maketh an
atonement for the soul" (Lev.17:11).

Chapter Seven

My Journey
Act As Though I Am Already,
There I Am

FROM PAIN TO POWER BY THE SPOKEN WORD

A QUOTE FROM: Apostle Julia 1/30/21, "All unhappiness comes from lack of spoken power, man imagines himself weak and a victim of circumstances claiming defeat. But linked with God's power of the Word, all things are possible. In my journey, the first word I hear in my abandoned spirit awakens my delivered heart, which now is very hard for me to comprehend. Only for this chapter of my book I must go back to collect by thoughts and dig deep to help others. I must visit these thoughts that have been destroyed by the love of my creator God the Father. Father I'm having difficulty trying to imagine what that looks like. Father help me Lord to continue this journey. I remember when I heard the song "Father" from the CD by Shekinah Glory. I was not able to relate and would pass by that song. Broken from abandonment, left in a home with my sister with no refrigerator, no stove in an abandon house with no life. We were all separated from each other, my oldest sister was with another uncle. I am not sure where my baby sister was located. What does abandonment mean? To be given up or to discontinue any further interest. To me, this meant to be left alone under the age of 6 years with a care giver who was only age 10. I remember my mother would show up with cooked food, only just enough for that moment with no leftovers, no refrigerator. I remember after the food was gone being hungry again. I would stand with my face pressed to window with tears in my eyes waiting for the next meal. I remember describing that my stomach was touching my back because it felt so empty. My response to this was when I grew up and became a mom, I would over protect and keep so much food in my refrigerator that sometimes the food would go to waste. We always had food. My children would laugh at me. Later, after retirement, my refrigerator was naked compared to their life with me. Hey, all this stuff is deep, when you are a child so much carries over into your adulthood. Have mercy on me Lord right now, this is too deep, but ok let's keep going. Lord for Your glory do we allow you to dig deeper. I am quite sure as I am 72 years young, I believe now that my wonderful young mom was discouraged and weary because she was suffering being abandoned. Her mother died when she was a young child. She was raised by her aunts with her two brothers and a sister in different homes also. Repeat of the attack of the enemy to destroy seeds of victory in the earth. My dad was incarcerated for defending himself in Conway, Arkansas. This was the first time I saw my dad. I was 32 years old when I found him. It was not the greatest experience, but it did fill the desire just to see him. When we arrived home, I was just fine, I had fulfillment in my heart. One day while my sister and I were living in the abandoned house that belonged to my mother's boy-friend's family, I received a huge box from my grandmother in Arkansas. It was so large that

I got inside to finish taking out the goodies. Oh my! so much food help my Lord had showed in great way. For some reason, I never forgot that box because I climbed over into it. I was unable to remember what my grandmother looked like. I was told that my grandfather was pure Indian and my dad was mixed, to me he look like an Indian. He was handsome and I am a female look alike. I always reminded my mother of him -- well that's another story. She was always negative and made me uncomfortable when she talked about my dad. I found my dad after starting my journey in nursing school. This action helped me to survive by closing the hole in my heart to prepare for my next level in life. My husband Ben drove us to Arkansas. I said that was not my greatest love connection I had experienced; but I was able to fulfill what I needed to go on after my leaving. We were connected for a short time. To tell you the truth, I don't do well with rejection to this day. I will keep it moving. I must stay in the presence of God with His love. In Him, I am able to love unconditionally, meaning for me need no return, all the glory to my creator God the Father. I believe that my mother relinquished her nurturing for us to place us in survival mode, keeping her daughters alive. Seeing this for the first time, as I put on her shoes, I found out that they are much too big for me. My children were never hungry with no lack because everybody worked in the house. I would say too much was handed to them. It makes me sad that I did the reverse. The journey continues, she was compelled to do what was acceptable at the time. I made it! Look at me now, a very accomplished, black, educated woman full of wisdom, knowledge, understanding and giving out sound counseling to all that are sent by God. I am a healthy black woman that He has created only for His glory. I remain in the hands of my heavenly Father, Elohim. Abandonment fears can impair a person's ability to trust others. Lord did I have trust issues; but who is rich in glory through Christ Jesus, sent me the most caring and loving boyfriend whom I married, and the greatest mother-in-law.

Merlin Lewis, who took me under wings and taught me everything I needed to survive. I still use those skills to this day. A shout out` to my beloved mother-in-law. She prophesied into my life for years. She told me that God would develop a strong relationship with my mom. I developed a great relationship with my mom until her death. We became close friends and after all the pain and hurt, God set me free. The spoken word is powerful. My mother-in-law declared my nursing career would manifest. She got me my first job at 16 years old as a nurse assistant at Bethesda Hospital. I thank God that He had a divine plan for my life from the start. Loneliness is not connected to my life. I can say in my youth, I believed I was suffering from loneliness, but now I have spent years leaning totally on the presence of the Almighty God, who I serve daily. I must say I love who I have become with much humility, so humble in the hands of my Lord. I am ready for the next adventure of my life with Him."

As I study this issue of abandonment, I realize I did fall into giving too much and being overly eager to please prior to allowing my God to control my life as my Lord and savior. Christmas at my house was "extra"- too much spending with too little return. I always received the least every Christmas. As a child I experienced so much lack at Christmas. I was the needy child on the block. I remember not having shoes and being unable to go to school at age six. I stood in the doorway of my uncle's apartment wishing that I could go to school. I was told that my mother did not love or care about me. I could only overcome that by learning as a young adult to love her unconditionally and forgive my past. Only God can heal abandonment issues. Lord help me, I was so humiliated by my peers, because I had on boy's tennis shoes. Now they are stylish for young girls; but back in my day you became the laughingstock of the class, being subjected to ridicule. Look at me now (I know I still need healing) I have too many shoes to count, too many to wear. Blessed by the best, I remain in the hand of my Creator, one second at a time, being molded for the Master. I see the appearance dawning when hurt arises from my past. I feel like I'm being attacked by my siblings -- a feeling of being an out-cast. I thank the Lord for His healing power. Feelings of unworthiness kept me thanking Him for my inspiration in His presence. I believe that Father God has rescued me in my brokenness. He came by His Holy Spirit and began to give me that comfort, attention in meditation, and has never left me lonely. He deposits joy down in my belly for me to use when necessary. My Holy Father is so awesome to me. Down in my soul I want to continue to the end, never turning back to that broken woman who needed her family to validate her. No insecurity can be found in this new woman, so secure in whose I am. Emotionally, my mind is totally fixed on my faith in the spoken word of God and His Power. My Caregiver seems to be working overtime in consistent warmth, never leaving me in this season of restoration. He returns me back to my first love in obedience, to the place from where He called me. I am ready to do the impossible in Him. I give Him praise for the new day.

Broken, but I remain in His hand. He is molding and perfecting me into something that is perfect and complete, without defect or blemish, accurate and exact. The word perfected can also be used as a verb, you guess it, to make perfect for those things that concern Him. Glory to His name my Lord and Savior for this season I live. How can I write this book? Only my God can make me again in His arms. Only in His presence can I, a mortal vessel, know my principles, and seek my truth. Surely my foundation is stronger than my wounded mother in the hands her family. She is called perfection while sitting in His presence, not knowing what I am, who I am or even what to do or which direction to go. Only in His presence do we find peace in the mist of pain, sorrow and disconnection from those we love. Not confused, but just in a human state while in His presence. He has called her to stand before His people to address the condition of His earth. He allows them to find Him in the mist of sorrow, pain and disappointment to bring victory. Only God can see right and wrong behavior and the goodness or badness of my human character. Only God can restore all that was lost and maintain that restoration in fellowship with Him through words of truth. In this dimension of sorrow, being restored from the breaking of a part of me, my heart is healing as I write out of my soul. My God is able to hold me and see His own creation before the foundations of the world. He said, this plan I have for you. "For I know the thoughts that I think toward you, said the Lord, thoughts of peace, and not evil, to give you an expected end" (Jer. 29:11). Glory to His wonderful name. This word was prophesied by a young prophet when I was in prayer at Oasis of Love Fellowship church in 1997. God is so amazing. His words are so powerful when they are given by inspiration from God. They are eternal when God is speaking, every time this word is repeated to me. I always remember that young man yielding and speaking life into my destiny. **The power of the spoken word drives us into that wonderful place of purpose.**

Every step is ordered by my Lord, although I am blinded by my human nature and this world. I continue to stay focused. Yes! He sees all knows all, touches all, hears all. "God is our refuge and strength, a very present help in trouble" (Ps.46:1). Help! Yes humanity, we need His help to be able to be used for His glory in the place of peace and joy in the Holy Ghost. "I beseech you there, brethren by the mercies of God, that ye present your bodies a living sacrifice, holy acceptable unto God, which is your reasonable service" (Rom. 12:1). What can we say of these things that our Lord has instructed, dying daily has been a task for me, not always catching the wind the of the Spirit with confidence. I believe this truth, that I can rely on His presence. I firmly trust and believe this is where I live, just holding on to His manifested presence, I move and continue to have my being. In this place where He works with us while in His hands, do we find that peace to continue to truly rely on our Holy Spirit to lead and guide us to all truth. We say yes to you Lord and remain in a position of yielding and responding by faith to that expected end. This is the day that the Lord has made and I am really glad, for this is a wonderful day of victory.

HOLDING ON!

Father, in the name of Jesus, let us give Him thanks that we are the head not the tail, that we are above and not beneath, we are well and not sick, and we have no lack in our lives. We are divinely blessed in every area of our lives through Christ Jesus whom restored us back to Elohim. Amen

Chapter 8

Walking In Victory

CHANGE YOUR WORDS/ CHANGE YOUR WORLD

Your word is your world. You are deliberately making a change in your life. Yes, let's reveal this awareness in the earth. We are living in this life on purpose. This is a plan from heaven. Write the vision down and make it plain. "And the Lord answered me, and said, Write the vision, and make it plan upon tables, that he may run that readeth it" (Hab.2:2). When words are written down and implemented, those that lead can run with us and that is when we see success. Writing the vision gives you the correct directions. You must follow to get to your destination. This is where you get inspiration and motivation, when God allows you to see past the tough challenges. Our vision must be made plain and clear in view. We must be in position to listen. Get in God's presence alone with Him. This will open you up to hear His voice plainly. Then write what is impressed in your heart as you are in His presence. If you receive inspiration, don't hesitate to keep moving forward. Believe in yourself to obtain victory, making it plain to understand as you move forward. Show a readiness to complete, be willing to pay the price it takes for completion. This will energize all who read the vision. Post it for all to see as a reminder to keep everyone motivated. Remember, there will be some obstacles; but we must hold to the vision God has set before us. The enemy came to steal. "The thief cometh not, but for to steal, and to kill, and to destroy: I am come that they might have life, and that they might have it more abundantly" (John 10:10). If we are focused on abundant life, the vision will manifest itself in God's time. Hold on to the promises of God and don't give up. Please do not rush your vision and start making your own plans. This will cause delay or even detour your destiny. All visions manifest in God's timing. We must have faith to believe that it is the plan of God, holding on your integrity at all cost, believing with commitment for the long hall. God's word will not return void, the more we are involved with the vision, the stronger the vision will become.

CHANGING YOUR WORDS CAN CHANGE YOUR MIND:

Today is the day of the Lord because He has called me today in my right mind to change how I think about me. Thankfully, learning how to move in a positive mindset has brought me to a different approach of deliberating -- changing the way I use words. I choose to use them daily to change how I think about my world. Changing my mindset is ordained by God in my new season. There are changes in my heart to walk in total deliverance if I can. When we change our words, when we transform our mindset, when we examine our beliefs, we will change our focus and we will begin to change our world. No matter what words you use, make sure you own them. Say them with conviction. The way to do that is to get out of your head and realize it does not matter what you say, but how you say it. As we speak these powerful words there is a change in our mind. Words can influence us, inspire us, or just as easily bring us to tears.

Words change our relationships, our demeanor, our entire system of beliefs, and even our businesses. The power of the positive word is peace and love. This strengthens areas in our frontal lobes and promotes the brain's cognitive functioning. The positive word propels the motivation center of the brain into action, according to the authors, and builds resiliency. Words can change your brain-psych central (STICKS AND STONES MAY BRAKE YOUR BONES, BUT WORDS CAN CHANGE YOUR MIND). That's right. According to Andrew Newberg M.D. and Mark Robert Waldman, words can literally change your brain.

Our focus is on our journey, watch as well as pray, to fulfill our purpose. We must keep our spiritual life strong by staying connected to God with our focus on prayer, praise, worship and meditation. The Lord has mandated that I should turn off TV and allow Him to shift my life to total surrender at this time. I have had this experience before in 2011, when I worked on a crusade with Apostle Charles. We were divinely focused totally on God and many miracles, signs and wonders occurred right in the midst of the Glory. One night I was working the alter, the next day this young lady was so excited, she walked up to me and said "see...see". I was confused as to why she was saying "see". She continued to tell me the night before she was blind and I had laid hands on her and now she could see. Glory to God we saw these type of miracles for 15 weeks on Dunn Road in North county in Saint Louis Mo. **We give God honor for all He showed us during that time of glory in His presence. God's words have creative power, He created new eyes for this young lady.**

Our physical health is extremely important for survival. My testimony is where the enemy attacked me in my health. I was short of breath for months taking an inhaler that was making me breath worse. In prayer, I received an impressive desire to stop using the inhaler. I stopped using it and watched my body closely. As a nurse, I knew how to monitor my breathing. I have been off this

24 hour inhaler since last year glory to God and His creative healing power. I declare healing now in the powerful name of Jesus Christ. "Gentle words bring life and health, a deceitful tongue crushes the spirit" (Prov.15:4); "Kind words are like honey- sweet to the soul and healthy for the body" (Prov.16:24). "A person words can be life giving water; words of true wisdom are as refreshing as a bubbling brook" (Prov.18:4). We must participate in the plan of God, taking care of our health is priority for me. As an RN, knowing the risk involved in health issues, eating heathy, using essential oils and taking vitamins is a part of good health care, including heart healthy exercise. Drinking water is a must to keep your kidneys flushed out. **We declare divine healing now, as you read this book my hope is that I will increase your faith to trust the Lord more for your healing.**

Walking strongly by faith is a mandate from our Lord, trust and believe it is impossible without Him. "But without faith it is impossible to please him for he that cometh to God must believe that he is, and that he is a rewarder of them that diligently seek him"(Heb. 11:6). This scripture speaks for itself. We must depend on our Lord to survive. In His will are His promises manifest. When we ask, believe. "And all things, whatever ye shall ask in prayer, believing, ye shall receive" (Matt. 21:22). Faith creates expectancy, ask with great expectations, continue to walk in truth. Love your neighbor and love yourself. **Walk in forgiveness and hold no man responsible, give all situation unto Our Lord.** "But if ye forgive not men their trespasses, neither will your Father forgive your trespasses" (Matt. 6:15). Walking in forgiveness will allow you to speak positive about others, even if they are unjust. We always speak positive words of encouragement. Truth gives us a sense of freedom; soon thereafter, actual freedom will follow which is required for the external. Continue to speak positively concerning any situation that is connected to you. **Victory is the promise of God in this journey.**

Chapter 9

Follow The Word

ENTHUSIASM

As we follow the Word of God, we are energized. We see now and what is to come by faith as we believe God. We are intensely and eagerly enjoying our journey. My expectation for my tomorrow is very interesting to me. Making the most of my disappointments, I turn them into hopeful moments. I wait on the Lord. "Since the beginning of the world men have not heard, nor perceived by ear, neither hath eyes seen, Oh God, beside thee, what he hath prepared for him that waited for him"(Isa.64:4). Change all failures into success while you wait by faith. Change all unforgiveness into forgiveness and all injustice to justice. Perfecting your life is an ongoing task. Get out of the rut of negative speaking and thinking which leads to negative living. That will keep you busy seeking God for the answers. For therein is the righteousness of God revealed from faith to faith. As it is written, the just shall live by faith (Rom. 10:6). The words say from faith to faith and glory to glory. Enthusiasm is defined as intense, eager enjoyment, interest and approval to be inspired or possessed by God. Enthusiasm is divine fire and kindles enthusiasm in others. If you lose your drive the fire goes out and no one else will keep up with your vision. Let's be enthusiastic about our spirit within and get up early to open our mind. Since I started writing again, I have been getting up at 5am and writing until the excitement lets me go. When I wake up, I am eager to begin my new day. Feeling great in my body is a plus from my Lord. I continue to bless the name of my Jesus all day. I give Him praise for my divine health. It is absolutely wonderful, inspiring down in my soul -- I just want to thank you Lord. He has perfect love toward His creation. I feel so much love as I seek Him early in a new beginning and new realm of Glory. From my Lord yes, I believe in miracles. Waiting for the divine plan of my life to be revealed in truth gives me a sense of freedom, soon we will see. It is divine activity in our bodies that bring health, wealth and peace. There are so many testimonies that we will allow some time at the end of my book to encourage God's people to hold on until He returns. But let's keep it moving in His presence while we are waiting for that great day of His return hoping He finds us doing His perfect will.

OBEDIENCE IS BETTER THAN SACRIFICE

"Behold, to obey is better than sacrifice, and to hearken than the fat of rams" (1 Sam.15:22). We as believers should do nothing to impress each other, but should all serve our Savior. We should speak positive words to shine a light upon our savior Jesus Christ who died for our sins and rose on the third day for our redemption. This is a selfless walk and is a totally yielded mind-set to serve our Lord and savior. "For many are called but few are chosen" (Matt.22:14). For to identify as chosen is divine obedience to our Lord. We are now going to discuss the Story of King Saul in 1 Samuel 15.

"Samuel said unto Saul, the Lord sent me to anoint thee King over his people, now therefore hearken thou unto the voice of the words of the Lord" (1 Samuel 15:1). Pay close attention to this story. Samuel warned the King and gave him instructions from the Lord that there is no excuse for disobedience when your instructions are presented clearly and plain. He was told everything that God said. In His word, God has made it clear that the Holy Spirit would reveal the deep things of God. Then Saul got the people together (v4); And Saul came to a city of Amalek, and laid wait in the valley (v5). Saul attacked the Amalekites (v7); and he took Agag the king of Amalekites alive, and utterly destroyed all the people with edge of sword. (v8) But Saul and the people spared Agag, and the best of sheep, and of oxen, and of the fatlings, and the lambs and all that was good, and would not utterly destroy them but destroyed the vile.(v 9). Then came the word of the Lord unto Samuel, the Lord will reveal to the prophet what is really going on in the camp. Watch king Saul try to lie and cover up the lie blaming the people. The Lord came to Samuel and told him everything. Saul knew that he was not to spare the enemy and surely not to collect the best for himself, then he had the nerve to spare the enemy. I believe this was from hidden pride. Beware of the hidden pride in your heart. Pride makes you want to look great in the eyes of God's people. After being confronted, Saul blamed the incident on the people knowing what Samuel said the Lord commanded. It repentant me that I have set up Saul to be king for he is turned back from follow me (v.11). When we don't obey what God said we are no longer following Him. **TO FOLLOW IS TO OBEY GOD.** The Lord sent thee on a journey and said, go and utterly destroy the sinners the Amalekites, and fight against them until they be consumed. (v. 18). He did not obey the voice of God (v.19) And Saul said unto Samuel yea, I have obeyed the voice of the Lord, and have gone the way which the Lord sent me But the people took of spoil, sheep and oxen the chief of the things which should have been destroyed, to sacrifice unto the Lord thy God in Gilgal (v.20-21). Wrong sacrifice for wrong reasons do not work in service unto the Lord, we should always obey the voice of the Lord. The perfect sacrifice is needed to please our Lord. Samuel said you gave burn offerings but failed to obey his command. Behold, to obey is better than sacrifice, and to hearken than the fat ram (v.22). For rebellion is as the sin of witchcraft, and stubbornness is as iniquity and idolatry. Because Thou hast rejected the word of the lord, he hath also reject thee from being king (v.24). Now therefore, I pray thee, pardon my sin, and turn again with me, that I may worship the Lord (v. 25). Saul was aware of damage of his disobedience, but he still rebelled thinking he could get away with his actions. We can't blatantly disobey God and walk back into His presence on our own terms. The Lord had rent the kingdom of Israel from thee this day, and hath given it to a neighbor of thine, that is better than thou (v. 29). God always has a plan to get all glory in His kingdom. He will use the willing obedient heart to do His will. We must be very concerned about our leadership style and who we follow because the oil rolls off the head of each leader. Follow only those that follow Christ. **There are consequences of lack of true repentance: rejection by God, Spiritual and physical death and loss of eternal glory.**

Chapter 10

Let's Talk

Why where we created?

The purpose of this chapter is to reveal His character and nature, and to provide for what God has made. Humanity's use of creation must promote not compromise but the ability of creation to reveal God and provide for humans and other creatures on the earth now and in the future. For what purpose were we created? We were created to give glory in the earth and assist as willing vessels to work the kingdom of God in the earth. We are to praise, revere, and serve God our Lord and by doing so, save our souls. We are to work, create, excel and be concerned about world affairs. Make an impact on the environment. Purpose is the reason you get up in the morning. Purpose can guide life decisions, influence behavior, shape goals, offer a sense of direction, and create meaning. For some people, purpose is connected to vocation, a job -- meaningful, satisfying work.

"So God created man in his own image, in the image he him, male and female created he them" (Gen1:27). This implies that

God has ownership over our lives and will one day justly pass eternal judgement upon us.

In Genesis, First God "said", then God "called". A statement called is a command after He said "let there be..". I just say Glory to His power in that it brought forth creation from His mouth. Then in the next verses, God set meaning- but in proper placement with His word. When He set out to lay or stand something in a specified place or position, He was placing them in order for us. What's important and what is not. That statement made me think more about the importance of us watching our words. I reflected on the words that awakened me this morning. They were "let's talk, my Lord want to talk". I give glory to His wonderful name. Man was created with the supernatural power of God. Then man fell from grace after disobeying God. Next, God revealed Himself through Jesus (Matt.14:28-29) and Peter answered him and said, Lord if it be thou, bid me come unto thee on water (v.29). And He said, come. And when Peter was down out of the ship, he walked on water, to go to Jesus.(v. 30). But when he saw the wind boisterous, he was afraid, and beginning to sink, he cried, saying, Lord save me (v.31). And immediately Jesus stretched forth his hand and caught him and said unto him, O thou of little faith, wherefore didst thou doubt? the wind ceased when they got back into the boat (v.32). Peter was able to walk on water as long as he was focused on Jesus. When he looked at the wind, he became afraid even though Jesus had already stated be not afraid. We must believe the words of Jesus. This is the plan of salvation, believing in the word. The Word is true and keeps us from fear by trusting and believing the word of God through his Son Jesus, the door of our salvation. And Peter said Lord is it you commanding me to come on the water? Then Jesus said come. Who am I that my Lord would choose to set me in a place to talk? He positions me for what I am called to do. I seek Him for the next wave of His Glory. He will reveal His secrets when I am called to walk in revelation.

This is the divine or supernatural disclosure to humans of something relating to human existence or the world. Words have power for both righteous and unrighteous purpose. "Death and life are in the power of the tongue" (Prov.18:21). The right word spoken at the right time carries tremendous force. A prophetic word can change a life. **Words drop like rain in your inspired spirit.** Words bubble up in the inspired spirit, out of the spirit flows living water. "He that believeth on me, as the scripture hath said, out of his belly shall flow rivers of living water" (John 7:38).

Revelation of The Supernatural God

Shifting into a great place of awareness of who I am. Revelation is the knowledge of God revealed to our spirits and it is by spiritually seeing, hearing and perceiving. We need structure as revealed in the book of Genesis. The revelation of the kingdom produces spiritual knowledge of how to use the authority of God and submitting to His authority. Without this knowledge we are destroyed. The bible states that we are destroyed from the lack of knowledge, In Hosea it says, "My people are destroyed for lack of knowledge because thou hast rejected knowledge". It goes on to say, "I will also reject thee, that thou shalt be no priest to me: seeing thou hast forgotten the law of thy God, I will also forget thy children" (Hos.4:6). This blesses me because my testimony is that when my son Maurice received his impartation, the first things he did was to seek God. He set a prayer closet then anointed his children for safety. Oh, how great our Lord is to train a young father how to protect his seed. He was being a priest. As lovely stones build up a spiritual house, a holy priesthood offers up spiritual sacrifices, acceptable to God by Jesus Christ. Also, Let's talk about rejecting knowledge. When you as a Christian, intentionally do not prepare to learn or put other things in place of bible study to avoid Sunday school. I believe people think if they don't know truth that they can avoid judgement. Well, we have no bible for that. We have been blessed with a sound mind and free will. Now there is a supernatural gift of knowledge that we will address later.

"And that ye put on new, which after God is created in righteous and true holiness" (Ephesians 4:24). Holiness comes straight from God -- not I but the Christ with in me. We are filled with the power of God and yielded to His eternal plan. Then as a result of your mind set, you are positioned in Christ the risen One. You are able to walk in holiness through the grace of God, by the power of the Holy Spirit who lives and dwells in you. Holiness is imputed to us by God because of Jesus Christ, the redeemer's work of the cross. "Sanctify yourselves therefore and be ye holy: for I am the Lord your God" (Lev. 20:7). This command was given to the priest and God's people to command His children to prepare for His atonement. The goal in the Old Testament was for the high priest to make it to the throne room. Our desire is to make to heaven. It is our desire to make it into the presence of God -- heaven on earth. Being holy is putting into practice what we learn, emulating Him in our actions, words, and character. Allowing the wisdom of God that has been threaded into our character to manifest into a new and improved character to be used for His glory. This is not a dress code or a voiced statement but truly a life of loving God and His people. This is a lifestyle presented in the earthen vessel. We are called to live holy and blameless before God. Desire His presence more than anything else so that we can be like Him, in character and in actions. The more we are in His presence, healing manifest and growth in our commitment to the call to His Kingdom is revealed responsibility. Loving and obeying God to live holy is increased. Accountability is revealed in His presence. So how do we define holiness? It is without blemish, complete, full, without spot, undefiled and upright. Holy is He. No sin is allowed in His presence. The holiness of God are His standards. Our complete obedience to God is not optional. The holiness of God makes no allowance for sin. That is why He sent His son Jesus that we may receive the Holy Spirit with power to yield and submit to Him. That through Him, we may walk in the power of God to develop the character of God and to manifest the holiness of God. May He get Glory out of our lives. **God is never unfair, He is always just**. We learn that we can trust God in His word to be true, fair and just when He needs to discipline us. This is the main puzzle piece to living through the discipline of God.

"And have put on the new man, which is renewed in knowledge after the image of him that created him" (Colossians 3:10). **Lack of knowledge is no order**. Order will never be established in the absence of governmental authority. We need God's authority in our lives to walk in His supernatural power. We need vision, which we detailed earlier in my writings. We need to know the purpose of why we were created in His image. Knowledge and revelation of the kingdom must be first in our lives. Knowing without this power would never be able to succeed in His will for our lives. Revelation allows us to suddenly understand something without the aid of natural sense. This knowledge or understanding can be given only by the Holy Spirit. "Flesh and blood has not revealed this to you, but my Father who is in heaven" (Matt. 16:17). In this quote, Jesus asked a question and the Almighty God revealed the answer to Peter. Jesus blessed Peter and acknowledge truth had been revealed. Jesus' blessings came to Peter first then He acknowledged Peter and declared with truth no hell can come against truth. And He gave Peter the keys to victory to bind and loose in heaven. This word was given to me in 1997 at the Azusa conference in Tulsa. Unto today, I remember that encounter as it changed my life. My prophetic birth was through Prophetess Pam Vinnett. She was teaching and I could not stop the tears from flowing, so being lead she imparted in my spirit the gift that the Lord had waited for me. Lord help, that I may continue in truth and knowing that heaven speaks to earth. Now He has given to me that I can speak from heaven, true revelation. Positioned by God in heavenly places in Christ Jesus. Blessed be the God and Father of our Lord Jesus Christ, who hath blessed us with all spiritual blessing in heavenly places in Christ. Amen

To receive revelation from God is to see as He sees, to hear as He hears, and to perceive as He perceives, "And he carried me away in the spirit to a great and high mountain and shewed me the great city, the holy Jerusalem, descending out of heaven from God" (Rev. 21:10).

Revelation includes knowing things you otherwise would not know, seeing things that have yet to occur, and perceiving without prior knowledge. This is the mind of God. This brings to my mind the gift of prophecy in operation, which reveals the heart and mind of God into the earth realm. It releases His supernatural results, with miracles manifest in His will. This the divine knowledge of a prophetic message. Such a message is given by inspiration, interpretation or revelation of divine will concerning the social world and events to come. See Revelation 9. **For the testimony of Jesus is the spirit of prophecy**. It is important that we stay connected to the Holy Spirit in prophecy. The word of God provides safety and protection from misuse and abuse of prophecy. God wants to use His word of truth to make our way prosperous and to cause us to walk in good success. Through the Holy Spirit we can recognize and know the voice of the Lord. In this mode, it is extremely important to be very aware of your words. **Please do not give a false or selfish report for own personal gain.** Prophecy is referring to hearing the voice of the Lord and speaking His word to others. Every believer that is filled with the Holy Spirit has the ability to operate in the prophetic realm, we all should hear the voice of God through the power of the Holy Spirit, all of us need more faith in order to flow in the prophetic. Do not allow the trauma of one season to prevent you from receiving the victories in your life. Allow the Holy Spirit to govern your spirit and allow your flesh to die. WE DECLARE IN THE MIGHTY NAME OF JESUS! THAT YOU WILL NOT ALLOW THE TRAUMA OF YOUR LAST SEASON TO EFFECT HOW YOU PRESENT YOUR LIFE TOWARD YOUR NEXT SEASON. ALLOW GOD TO HEAL YOU NOW. WE DECLARE THAT OUR TRAUMAS OUR FEARS WILL NOT AUTHOR THE BOOK THAT GOD HAS DECLARED ABOUT OUR LIVES. NOW RECEIVE FREEDOM FROM HAZARD SEASONS MOMENTS OF DARKNESS, RISK AND WE DECLARE THAT WE WILL WALK IN DELIVERANCE AND FREEDOM TO RECEIVE AND EXPRESS THE WILL OF GOD FOR OUR LIVES NOW IN HIS NAME JESUS CHRIST. AMEN.

Revelation operates outside of time, space and matter. In the absence of progressive divine revelation, people like to criticize everything they can't create or understand "Which things also we speak, not in words which man's wisdom teacheth, but which the Holy Ghost teacheth" (1 Cor.2:13).

Who is that source of revealed knowledge?

The Holy Spirit, He is the only channel that gives us true access to God the Father our creator. He releases this revealed wisdom or knowledge. He hears what is said in heaven and repeats it to men and women on earth. We cannot know our creator God without the help of the Holy Spirit, "But the comforter, which is the Holy Ghost, whom the Father will send in my name, he shall teach you all things and bring all things to your remembrance, whatsoever I have said unto you" (John 14:26).

The natural senses alone cannot perceive the revealed wisdom or knowledge of God. However, these mysteries have already been revealed through the Holy Spirit (1Cor. 2:10-11). The human mind is not able to know everything that is in man. Only the Holy Spirit knows all things and knows that the only one who can reveal God is the spirit of God. It is useless to apply biblical terms while pursuing man made methods. The only way to know God and relate to His supernatural and invisible realm is by faith. "But without faith it is impossible to please Him; for He that cometh to God must believe that He is, and that He is a rewarder of them that diligently seek Him" (Heb.11:6). God will not reveal himself to those that lack the desire to know him or lack relationship with Him. "Nether cast your pearls before swine" (Matt.7:6).

God's revelations depend on His time and His will. Our faith will be elevated most in the areas which we have the greatest revealed knowledge from God. Whereas, we are weak in the areas that are lacking revelation. Therefore, lack of knowledge is where the enemy will establish his stronghold.

There are two realms: the natural and the supernatural. The natural is the dimension that is subject to the laws of time, space and matter. This is a dimension that can be accessed only through the physical senses. The Supernatural is the dimension that operates above natural laws, present, invisible and eternally located outside of time. It can be only access only by faith (2Cor.4:18).

Jesus is speaking, so we speak by faith

For thine is the kingdom, and power, and the glory, forever. The substance of Jesus teachings is the kingdom, through power and glory.

The kingdom is the government of God. It is the ability that is found in God through the Glory, that is the Divine presence of God. We need eternal peace to take us higher to those heavenly places in Christ Jesus. That secret place is where you have been drawing and knocking. My coming Lord, You take us into your manifested Glory in that place of communion. Talk to me Lord, where Your mysteries are unfolded, in that secret place to take us higher. Lord, that we may speak destiny and purpose as you see.

Only where you and I are Lord. This must be a personal walk right in the spiritual realm of your Holy God. Let's talk!

Encounters with the Lord are real.

There are two sources of the Supernatural Power: **Our Holy God** and Satan the thief

Any power not from God is considered from Satan. While I was pastoring at 104 S. Florissant Mo., we experienced numerous moves and encounters of God. We went to Literacy school through United Way and taught the members to read. We were trained in the after-school program and taught children in our district how to read. We worked strongly in our community seeing God move with children in needed situations. Children accepted Jesus as their Lord and savior. We received a word from the Lord to stay connected and placed a banner on the wall in our Sanctuary. Revelation of the power of connection to Him in prayer were the words given in prayer. We continued in prayer as the Lord had instructed. I was still working as an RN at the VAMC. Apostle Maurice would show up and another move of Glory to the next dimension would appear. I left to go to my job as an RN. It was a glorious time in the Lord with our Apostle in the house teaching about the Glory of God. God's people were hungry and stayed for another service. There was so much honor given in that presence. The prophetic was in our house from 2002-2003 with miracles, signs and wonders following healings. Our musicians were called by God to lay on hands. They could hear the sounds, then played in the Spirit creating Glory. Prior to moving, we created a CD and I developed a recording company. I was CEO and co-producer of The Message which had been sent through God's messengers. We traveled throughout the surrounding cities, counties, Illinois and Texas to bring young people to Christ.

Always taking time to judge the power by the word of God, His presence filled the room when they were filled with His power source -- the Holy Ghost. "And when they had prayed, the place was shaken where they were assembled together; and they were filled with the Holy Ghost, and they spoke the word of God with boldness" (Acts 2:3). As we performed the CD, God always used that platform to teach how to minister salvation, and holy boldness. We continued to say and operate in a holy environment. Outreach was the foundation of our ministry and we are building now on the power of the spoken word.

Not Jesus' will, but will of the Father who sent Him. Jesus said to obey His word by redeeming His people back to the heart of God. Jesus said in the book of John, "This is the Father's will which hath sent me, that of all which he hath given me I should lose nothing, but should raise it up again at the last day" (John 6:39). Thank You Lord. Nothing is lost in Jesus.

Testimonies of Apostle Byas
& Immanuel Temple -God With Us

B irth Immanuel Temple- God with us in prayer 2000 praying for one year, many miracles occurred during this time @ 8786 North Broadway started pastoring in the basement at 10370 Halls Ferry Road on September 9, 2001.

We will give a few of the testimonies in our walk from pain to power.

In prayer in the year 2000 we had a husband come into the sanctuary and fell to his knee, crying and stated he had left his gun outside came to shoot his wife but was not able to bring the gun inside. Miracles do occur in the presence of God.

We had a husband & wife in combat against each other came to prayer they were seeking a divorce, their marriage was restored, received deliverance and are now parents and pastoring the church of God in Missouri. Nineteen years later. To God be all the glory for this couple and their family.

We experience a women that was filled with demonic spirits, cast out in prayer, found out that there was activity in her home sent 2 elders to her home to rid of items that she had obtained and her deliverance was complete.

Julia Byas was in Deaconess Hospital in ICU in 2000 with chest pain etiology unknown after saying yes to the Lord with much difficulties, was removed out of ICU and started on her journey as pastor with no cardiac damage 20 years later YES Lord. In 2020 Apostle Julia suffered with respiratory problem received instruction in prayer from the Holy Spirit, lead her to stop taking the 24-hour inhaler that was causing the problem she was healed from asthma as the doctor was trying to convince her but not receiving this diagnosis led her to believe God she has been freed and doing well lost excess weight doing well and walking in Devine health. Thank You Lord.

We received a word from the Lord September 15, 2002 Upon this Church the Glory of God is manifested this day. This is the day that the Lord has made. I am the same, God today and yesterday forever more said God, hold on to my unchanging hand said God. I will do a new thing in your life if it is not true, I would not have said it. This is the day This is the day, A new day said God. We have seen the Glory of God every time we inter in. During the pandemic we are able to keep our doors open keeping within the guidelines of social distancing wearing mask at nearing the end of 2020 until we had an addition to our sanctuary our place of refuge and safety God is faithful, no one is sick no jobs lost our income increased in our sanctuary. We received increase as individuals in our income. I was instructed to administer communion every Sunday, including children some of our children parents that do not attendant our church their grandparents bring them. Parents had the virus, but the children were covered. In our congregation we have nurses, childcare workers and hospital staff in our church we continue to obey God using our vitamins and essential oil that we started in 2017 and God has covered us with his grace and mercy. We give him all the Glory.

2016 December/2017 January a young lady in her 20's joined our church went to college in New York and could not complete her college degree due to financial problem. As her church family we all supported her to come back home. She returned and was able to start her own business as a church body we lent her the money to obtain the car, I was able to find her a used car she was strengthen. She was catching the bus with her case with supplies that she used for her cleaning business. We as a group went to credit counseling and got our credit together, the seven hundred club a move of God for all that attended. God gave her strength and we gave her support to start a successful business. She met her soul mate and got married and later was able to buy two brand new car with her husband, they both were able to give God glory He is so good. From defeat, pain and sorrow to victory from her pain to sorrow. She paid the church back and truly received victory revealed as a Mighty Women of God.

In 2017 we experienced so many miracle we had a young 25 year old young man an alcoholic staggered into the church, mental problem and was living on park benches unemployed and needed salvation God saved and filled with His Holy Spirit, delivered him he got a job drug free and obtain his freedom got married and became financially stable.

In 2017 A young male in his twenties, who was raised in the church, came to us suicidal after a tragic experience. God set him free he became stable, served excellently well in Immanuel Temple God with Us and was able to obtain his hearts desires from after a high school desire and fulfilled his destiny completing his education and life serving the Lord.

We experienced a mother of 2 homeless and she received her deliverance and her young teen and 9 years old received the power of the Holy Spirit and received housing started her own business and was able to obtain her heart's desire. She was featured in our black paper for her accomplishments. Words of defeat with changing our words power is manifested.

2018 I received a call from Mrs. M she was sent home from hospital with a terminal report damaged to gallbladder from an unknown fractured hip and I noticed that she looked septic on antibiotics not getting better had to have family to take her out of bed unable to walk. We prayed and she was healed instantly now walking in her victory with no complication. Truly God is a healer.

2020 Ben Isaiah was diagnosed with kidney problems set up to go to surgery with his unsaved grandmother in charged, but we declared no surgery and fasted with him no surgery. On the day of scheduled surgery, Apostle Julia was at the hospital and went into ultrasound to and verify as she had asked God for healing, repeat showed kidney size had changed no surgery. Ben was filled with the Holy Spirit @ age 5. He is now attending Lane University and grade point average 3.8 on full ride a scholar, he is 19 years old with excellent health and attending chapel weekly. We give God glory for Ben a prophet at ITGWU when he entered kindergarten, he spoke into his own life at age 6 years old, that he would attend college. To God be all glory now. Words true to power of the manifest of the will of God.

In January 2021 Mr. T was scheduled to go to California to attend college was filled with the Holy Spirit, on that Sunday went to play basketball and had a terrible accident, He called Apostle Julia, while in ambulance lacerations and fractured ankle open wound bleeding, he was in good spirit no pain the MS employees could not understand why he was not in pain. He told Apostle that, as he was falling, he saw a vision of himself running down the court in full form, then he held on to the vision. No pain in ER the staff could not explain pain free with this type of injury. It was the power of God. He had received the power of the Holy Spirit with the evidence of speaking in tongues that Sunday morning. He did not lose his scholarship that is another miracle. He is now in college in rehab and enjoying and doing well, we at ITGWU started a college fund for his housing. God is working with Mr.

T. By faith we give this testimony today. His report is that he has healed exceptional well per his Ortho doctor. Walking without support of brace or crane. We say our healer is on the scene.

Today he is still in college playing ball; to God we give the Glory!

This year we have seen people come into our classes not been able to read or express themselves and received deliverance. Able to speak in public, hear when they could not hear spiritually and even one obtain healing from not hearing even with earing aid can hear now. Except the call of God on their lives and walk in the freedom in God. We are so thankful for being able to stay in our Sanctuary and stay connected in a place of refuge and safety, taking communion as we were lead in our knowing.

We remain to pray every Saturday@1pm and the Glory of God meet us in the building Mr. M was healed from liver cancer and has remained cancer free and is walking in his victory now. God continue to have us council him to keep him connected he is a devoted member preparing for Men's fellowship God has kept Mr. M in the mist of many storms he is truly a pioneer in our congregation. The Power of Word will set us free and continue to be a keeper. The Word of God will not return void in our faith.

WITH SO MANY WONERFUL TESTIMONIES, THESE ARE JUST A FEW, WE CONTNUE TO GIVE GOD ALL THE GLORY!

CPSIA information can be obtained
at www.ICGtesting.com
Printed in the USA
JSHW050955180222
23048JS00002B/67